Concurrent planning
Achieving early permanence for babies and young children

Sarah Borthwick and Sharon Donnelly

Published by
British Association for Adoption & Fostering
(BAAF)
Saffron House
6–10 Kirby Street
London EC1N 8TS
www.baaf.org.uk

Charity registration 275689 (England and Wales) and SC039337
(Scotland)

British Library Cataloguing in Publication Data
A catalogue record for this book is available from the British Library

ISBN 978 1 907585 80 7

Project management by Jo Francis, Publications, BAAF
Designed and typeset by Helen Joubert Design
Printed in Great Britain by the Lavenham Press

BAAF is the leading UK-wide membership organisation for all those
concerned with adoption, fostering and child care issues.

Contents

Notes about the authors

Sarah Borthwick is an independent social work trainer and consultant. She provides training for social workers and managers, foster carers and adoption and fostering panel members. She chairs an adoption and permanence panel for a local authority and three fostering panels for two local authorities. She is a former chair of Brighton and Hove's adoption and permanence panel which recommends approvals of concurrent carers and prospective adopters. She is the co-author of two good practice guides, *Together or Apart? Assessing siblings for permanent placement* (2008), and *Effective Fostering Panels* (2011), both published by BAAF.

Sharon Donnelly was previously the Head of Service for Fostering and Adoption at Brighton and Hove City Council. She was involved in setting up and managing the concurrent planning team in Brighton and Hove which was the first such team based within a local authority. She has given a number of presentations at conferences on topics including concurrent planning, parent and child fostering and family and friends care. She is now working as an independent social work trainer and consultant and remains a member of the Brighton and Hove adoption and permanence panel.

Natasha Watson (co-author of Chapter 4) is the Managing Principal Lawyer for Brighton and Hove City Council and co-chair of the Sussex Family Justice Board. She was actively involved in the development of concurrent planning in Brighton and Hove and sat on the steering group. She has spoken at a number of national conferences on the legal framework for concurrent planning.

Darren Howe (co-author of Chapter 4) is a barrister practising at 1 Garden Court Family Law Chambers, specialising in family law and is also a Recorder "ticketed" to hear private and public law family proceedings. He also sits as a Deputy District Judge hearing civil proceedings, domestic violence and harassment cases and ancillary relief applications. Darren has also delivered lectures on such topics as adoption, care planning and the Public Law case management protocol and is a regular contributor to the *Family Law* journal.

Acknowledgements

We would like to thank the many concurrency adopters and families for their very helpful input and honest descriptions about what concurrent planning is really like – in particular, the Brighton and Hove concurrency adopters who gave up their time to come to meetings to talk about their experiences or who provided written accounts. Contributions have also been gratefully received from Coram concurrency adopters via the current research project being undertaken by the Policy and Research team at Coram.

We have been very fortunate to have had support and contributions from a number of different people who have shared their expertise and experiences. We are very grateful to Natasha Watson and Darren Howe for their authorship of the legal chapter within this guide. We would like to thank the following people who read the draft and gave invaluable comments and made suggestions: John Simmonds, Karen Devine, Jeanne Kanuik and Mary Beek. We would also like to thank others for contributing to the guide or sharing information, including Dr Sian Bennett, Vanessa Wright, Gill Grey, Sophie Laws, Rosemary Wolfson, Shabnam Rathore, Barbro Loader, Carol Norcott, Catrina Dickens, Priscilla McLoughlin, Tracy Mather, Carol Wassell and Terry Fitzpatrick. We would also like to extend our thanks to Margaret Adcock, who has been such a champion of concurrent planning for many years.

Thanks also to Jo Francis and Katrina Wilson from BAAF for their support and very helpful input.

Finally, a very special thanks goes to Kay Willmer and John Cuthbert.

1

Introduction

The primary focus of concurrent planning is to place a child, typically under two years of age, with carers who will be the child's foster carers while the local authority pursues its rehabilitation plan with the parents during care proceedings. Should adoption become the local authority's plan and the court makes a placement order, the carers become the child's prospective adopters and the placement becomes an adoption placement. The carers are therefore dually approved by either the local authority or a voluntary adoption agency as *concurrent carers*, i.e. as both foster carers and prospective adopters. They are fully prepared to both foster and adopt a child who is matched with them. Concurrent carers are required to be child-focused, whatever the eventual plan, and to be able to cope with a high level of uncertainty about the outcome of the placement. They often play a very active role in engaging with the birth parents during contact arrangements as part of the fostering phase. Intensive preparation, assessment and support are necessary.

Parents and birth families must be fully informed of the local authority's plans for both rehabilitation and adoption. There will need to be a clear set of expectations that the parents will address their difficulties in providing a safe and nurturing family life for the child. Proactive engagement, honest feedback and timely intervention by skilled workers and managers are essential. The primary purpose of concurrent planning is to ensure that the uncertainty for all the adults involved – parents, professionals and carers – does not directly impact on the child and ensures that the child has a single and stable placement throughout the evolution of the plan and proceedings. That placement will only change if it is decided that the right long-term plan for the child is for them to return to their parents or other family members.

Concurrent planning may take place in a number of situations and early identification of children for whom it is suitable is crucial. For example, concurrent planning may be appropriate for:

- infants and children where there is a small chance of rehabilitation and a strong likelihood of adoption. Rehabilitation is being actively assessed during the fostering phase.

- infants and children who are placed with their birth parent in parent and child fostering or residential placements. However, the prognosis is extremely poor and a concurrent placement for the child is a contingency plan.

- infants and children where there is virtually no chance of rehabilitation, given the parents' recently assessed difficulties. Rehabilitation is not being actively pursued by the local authority but the issues are still to be determined by the court.

Concurrent planning may also be appropriate for some infants and children who are voluntarily relinquished by their birth parents. There may be circumstances where a direct placement from hospital with a concurrent carer would be a suitable option, given the fact that they have been fully prepared and assessed to cope with uncertainty and rehabilitation is a possibility.

FOSTERING FOR ADOPTION (FfA)

The Government in England is seeking to widen the scope of concurrent planning through the introduction of fostering for adoption (FfA) (Department for Education, 2012c). The Government hopes that this, along with other reforms, will result in an increase in the numbers of children in care who achieve permanence via adoption and that such placements will take place at an earlier stage. In FfA, local authorities in England are being strongly encouraged to place children with prospective adopters who are also approved as foster carers. Moreover, the Children and Families Bill 2013, which is expected to be enacted in 2014, contains a clause setting out that such placements must be considered for every child where the local authority is considering adoption.

Such prospective adopters may already be dually approved, like concurrent carers, or they may be prospective adopters who are granted temporary approval as foster carers for a named child. A new regulation under the Care Planning, Placement and Case Review Regulations is being introduced enabling such temporary approvals (see regulation 25 (A) of CPPCR and Fostering Services (Miscellaneous Amendments) Regulations 2013 which comes into force on 1 July 2013). This regulation is supported by updated statutory guidance and online practice guidance available at www.coram.org.uk/section/Fostering-for-adoption-guidance.

As with concurrent planning, FfA aims to create continuity for carefully identified children, usually babies, who can be placed with foster carers who will go on to adopt them, if the court makes a placement order and the adoption agency agrees the match. FfA is intended for those children where the issues of concern in relation to the birth family are so significant that the local authority has determined that adoption is the likely plan and is not actively pursuing work towards rehabilitation. For example, FfA could be considered in cases where a child or other children born to the birth parents have recently been placed for adoption and there is no evidence of change or in cases where the birth parents and birth family have already been fully assessed as not being able to care for the child. As with concurrent planning, the dually approved carers will be expected to carry the burden of uncertainty during the fostering phase as there may be unexpected changes in the birth family situation and the child may be rehabilitated with a birth family member. The FfA carers will need to be assessed, properly prepared and supported in undertaking the fostering task. It is still for the court and only the court to authorise the plan for adoption when it makes a placement order. It is then for the adoption agency to approve the adoption placement of the children with the carers as prospective adopters.

FfA requires as much care, planning and resources as concurrent planning and many of the practice and legal issues set out in this guide will be relevant. It is important to note that FfA is an evolving and largely untested policy and practice development. Concurrent planning has been undertaken in parts of the UK since the late 1990s. There are many useful lessons and practice experience to draw upon for both FfA and future concurrent planning placements.

Concurrent planning is a challenging and complex area of work. There has been considerable suspicion and hostility about its use in both the social work and legal professions. Some professionals regard it as a short-cut to adoption without sufficient attention being given to the birth parents' position and needs (Dale, 2011). It is essential therefore that children's social workers and adoption and fostering social workers within local authorities and/or across agencies understand their respective roles and responsibilities. Children's social workers will need to be able to identify children, for whom concurrent planning is appropriate, at a very early stage in their contact with them. They will need to be able to refer such children to adoption and fostering social workers in the local authority or to a voluntary agency that provides concurrent carers. In most cases, this work will take place as care proceedings are being considered by the court. Everyone concerned will need a full understanding of the advantages, stages and challenges of concurrent planning. Lead managers will have to be identified who can champion the model and provide full support to its implementation. It is extremely important to maintain the reputation of concurrent planning as a service that primarily works to assist children and their parents rather than carers and professionals.

THE ORIGINS OF CONCURRENT PLANNING

Concurrent planning was originally developed in the USA and was defined in 1994 by Linda Katz *et al*, the pioneers of this model, as:

> *To work towards family reunification whilst at the same time establishing an alternative permanent plan.*

It meant that two plans for the child were developed and worked towards *at the same time* (Plan A and Plan B). The original US model was used in cases that were deemed to have a very poor prognosis, based on the severity of the parents' and family's difficulties. Time limits for parental reunification were set that prioritised the child's timescales and the urgency of decision making. Full disclosure of the concurrent care plan to all parties and agreement by the court were essential. Concurrent carers who could foster and adopt were recruited and prepared.

Plan A involved a clearly defined period in which a full assessment towards reunification took place, options were explored and decisions were reached to make recommendations to the court. Intensive work was undertaken with the parent(s). This included both assessment and support to establish whether the parent(s) were able to demonstrate the required and agreed changes to their behaviours and/or lifestyle needed to enable the child to return home. Workers also explored the possibility of placing the child with other members of the birth family. Good quality, regular contact between the child and family members was arranged, not only to enable workers to assess the quality of interactions and parents' abilities to change their behaviour, but also for the child to establish relationships with them. Plan B focused on providing a secure placement of the child with concurrent carers who would become the child's adopters if rehabilitation under Plan A was not possible.

The original projects in England adopted this model. Practice has continued to develop to include a wider range of situations.

KEY ELEMENTS OF CONCURRENT PLANNING

- **Early identification and assessment of the central problems that led to the infant or child being removed.** This involves an analysis of the strengths of the family as well as what would need to change to enable rehabilitation.

- **Full disclosure to all parties in the care planning process** and an emphasis on openness and honesty with the parents at the outset and throughout the process. This means:

- ensuring that the parents understand their legal rights and responsibilities;

- being very explicit with the parents about the key issues that led to the child's placement in care; the timeline for the assessment work; the support that will be available to them; the expectations of them; and the changes that are needed before rehabilitation can become a safe and effective plan;

- ensuring that the parents understand that their child is placed with foster carers who could become the child's adoptive parents if this becomes the plan. The parents will need to be reassured and reminded that it is not a competition between them and another set of parents;

- ensuring that the concurrent carers are very clear about their role and that the focus of the care plan is to work to place the child back with their parents if at all possible;

- ensuring that all other parties in the legal process are aware of the care plan and status of the placement.

- **Active consideration of the wider birth family,** including early determination of paternity where appropriate and identification of other people in the family network who might be able to provide a permanent family for the child if they are not able to return to their parents.

- **Clear agreements about contact for the child with their parents,** detailing the expectations of the parents in contact and how this will be kept under review. The role of contact within the assessment and the provision of parenting skills and advice work will need to be explicit within the contact agreement.

- **A focus on "behaviour not promises"** in relation to the expectations of the parents, with primacy given to the child's urgent need for security, stability and belonging.

- **Setting clear timelines for the decision making** and drawing up clear written agreements with the parents about what the expectations are of them, the focus of the assessment and support available.

- **Specific recruitment of concurrent carers.** The model brings with it the potential benefits of a relationship between the carers and birth family but there is a need for the provision of intensive support.

- **Provision of intensive support to birth family members,** if rehabilitation is the plan.

- **Provision of post-adoption support,** if adoption is the plan. As with many adoptions, some adoptive families and children will require periodic access to support services, depending on needs and circumstances.

- **A higher level of post-adoption contact is likely.**

DEMANDS OF CONCURRENT PLANNING

Concurrent planning places very significant demands on parents, concurrent carers and social workers. These cases involve children where there is a small chance of rehabilitation but the parents must be given a genuine chance of achieving this. Parents, carers and workers must therefore be very well supported to cope with the ambivalence and tensions concurrent planning entails. Parents and birth families will need to demonstrate their commitment and ability to change the circumstances in their lives that have led to them being unable to meet their child's needs. They will need to undertake significant work to achieve this. Concurrent carers will form secure attachments to young and highly vulnerable children whom they may or may not adopt. They will need to be matched carefully at a very early stage, when information about the child is often limited. They will usually be actively involved in contact arrangements between the child and the birth family, unless there are risks to their safety and/or that of the child. Where they can be involved, relationships between concurrent carers and the birth family will establish themselves through handover meetings at contact.

Although not a legal requirement, it is good practice that concurrent care plans are agreed by the court as part of care proceedings. The parents should be fully aware that their child is placed with carers who are able to adopt their child if rehabilitation cannot take place. Equally, the concurrent carers should be fully aware that work is being undertaken to pursue rehabilitation actively with the parents or wider birth family. Social workers, psychologists, psychiatrists, courts, lawyers, Children's Guardians, and all those playing a role in undertaking this work should be fully aware of the implications of a particular concurrent care plan.

GOVERNMENT'S ACTION PLAN AND PROPOSALS FOR ADOPTION REFORM IN ENGLAND

The Government's Action Plan for adoption re-emphasises the role that concurrent planning can play in achieving early permanence for very young children (DfE, 2012a). It outlines worrying statistics regarding delays in the system and their impact on children who are eventually placed for adoption. It notes that 3,450 children were adopted from care in England in 2011/12. Out of this number, only 60 were children under 12 months. The average time between entering care and moving in with their adoptive family for a very young child was one year and nine months. For children who entered care at two years and six months, the average time to placement for adoption was another two years and six months. Most children were subject to lengthy court proceedings lasting an average of 55 weeks (Family Justice Review Panel, 2011). The

Government has therefore set out a raft of measures to tackle delays in the system and reduce the impact of delay on children's development and life chances. These include introducing legislation that requires care proceedings to be completed within 26 weeks, unless there are exceptional circumstances. It also requires early permanent placements for all children wherever possible (see Children and Families Bill 2013).

The Government also recognises the particular role that concurrent planning can play:

> *Concurrent planning is a well-established process which can help provide early stability for children who may be adopted...Almost all concurrent planning placements have resulted in the baby being adopted by the carers with whom they have lived, in most cases, from just a few weeks of age. Concurrent planning means that children get a stable loving home as early as possible and that the risks of disruption are taken by adults rather than children.*

(DfE, 2012a, para 60)

The Government also recognises the complexity of concurrent planning:

> *Concurrent planning depends on front-line social workers being equipped to identify and refer on cases where concurrent planning may be appropriate. It places significant demands on the social workers and carers involved. They must work intensively with the birth family to give them the best chance of resolving the issues that led to the child coming into care. They must manage regular and appropriate contact between the child and the birth family to minimise disruption if the child does return home. Above all, the carers must be well trained and be able to cope emotionally and practically with the possibility that they may not go on to adopt the child in their care.*

(DfE, 2012c)

The Government goes on to state that concurrent planning is challenging but should be one of the options considered by all local authorities for their youngest looked after children.

The Government is also concerned about the numbers of children currently waiting to be matched and, at the time of writing, is consulting on whether to introduce legislation requiring some or all local authorities in England to outsource the recruitment and assessment of prospective adopters (DfE, 2013, and Children and Families Bill 2013). Local authorities and voluntary adoption agencies (VAAs) intending to develop concurrent planning will need to consider these proposals and explore the potential for partnership working in the recruitment and assessment of concurrent carers (see Chapters 6 and 8). The Association of Directors of Children's Services (ADCS) has responded to the Government consultation (see ADCS, 2013).

ADOPTION GUIDANCE

Concurrent planning is identified in the 2011 revision of the Adoption Statutory Guidance for England. Chapter 2 of the Guidance explains concurrent planning and comments on its use. It sets out that:

> ...concurrent planning is usually most appropriate when the child is under-two...It is not the right option for all children...But it should always be considered, in the context of care planning as a whole, as one of the possible options for achieving permanence for a child.

The Guidance goes on to state that:

1 *Local authorities should actively consider the advantages of concurrent planning and integrate the approach into their permanency planning arrangements delivered in-house or commissioned from another adoption agency. This may mean:*

- *training and supporting permanency planning teams and fostering and adoption panels to use the model;*

- *integrating concurrent planning into care planning protocols;*

- *dually preparing, supporting and approving foster carers/prospective adopters;*

- *agreeing local court protocols to support concurrent planning; and*

- *making support and rehabilitation services available in a timely way for parents.*

CONCERNS ABOUT CONCURRENT PLANNING

Concerns have been expressed that concurrent planning inevitably leads to the adoption of young children, and it has been seen as a "back door" route to adoption. It is argued that parents' rights and opportunities are given scant regard and scarce resources diverted away from appropriate treatment programmes (Dale, 2011). However, this should not be the case. Concurrent planning must take place in the context of proactive care planning and court proceedings where parents are fully represented. It will be used in those cases where there is already a poor prognosis and a strong likelihood of adoption as the most likely plan in the child's long-term interests. The areas of concern in relation to the parents and birth family will already be clearly identified, fully documented and of a significantly high level. Moreover, it is only when, and if, assessments demonstrate that the parents and birth family cannot care for their child that placement orders will be made by the court and the local authority authorised to make an adoption placement.

WHY THIS GUIDE?

This good practice guide aims to assist social work practitioners, managers, medical advisers, contact supervisors, Children's Guardians, lawyers, the courts and all those who are or who plan to become involved in concurrent planning. It focuses on a range of different situations where concurrent planning can be considered. The guide draws on messages from practice undertaken by a number of projects in England and the US, both in the past and currently. Particular reference is made to work undertaken by Brighton and Hove City Council and by Coram in partnership with a number of local authorities. Past lessons from other projects, including the Goodman project in Manchester and Kent County Council, are also discussed. The guide focuses mainly on practice in England undertaken within the English legal framework. However, it includes discussion about many areas of good social work practice. It is hoped therefore that the guide should be relevant and useful to practitioners across the UK.

The guide is structured in the following way.

- **Chapter 2** sets out the research that focuses on the need for early stability and secure attachment for children's development. It also outlines some key messages regarding appropriate and successful interventions with parents. It looks at the success rate of reunifications and the practice of making decisions to separate children from their parents. The experiences for infants during contact are considered and adoption outcomes explored.

- **Chapter 3** covers the history of concurrent planning in both the US and UK. It explores the development of concurrent planning and its widened definition. It outlines learning points from practice experience and sets out key messages to consider for implementation.

- **Chapter 4** explains the legal framework for concurrent planning in England. It covers the legal requirements for practice from care application to final care plan. The principles of concurrent planning are reinforced from both a legal and social work perspective. Challenges raised about the use of the model in court proceedings are fully explored and relevant case law is detailed.

- **Chapter 5** focuses on the child's concurrent care plan pathway. This includes pre-birth assessment work and early identification of appropriate children and parents for whom concurrent planning could be considered. It outlines the need to assess other birth family members and emphasises the importance of family group conferences early in the process. It covers matching considerations and includes a section on the role of the agency medical adviser. This chapter describes the transition of the care plan from concurrency to rehabilitation or adoption and includes the role of the local authority adoption panel.

- **Chapter 6** focuses on the recruitment, assessment, supervision and support of concurrent carers. It covers the additional essential elements that need to be addressed in preparation and assessment. The key role played by concurrent carers' supervising social workers is highlighted.

- **Chapter 7** outlines the role contact plays during the assessment of rehabilitation, the involvement of concurrent carers and parents and their support needs. It explores the impact of contact on infants and outlines lessons from relevant research in more detail. It sets out a number of good practice points to be considered when developing contact plans and undertaking contact arrangements in practice.

- **Chapter 8** sets out key pointers for local authorities and VAAs in assessing the viability of introducing and implementing concurrent planning, given the needs of children and families in their areas. It outlines a number of models for delivery and discusses implementation issues. Examples of local authority and VAA sole services and partnerships are provided.

- **Chapter 9** concludes the guide and re-emphasises the Government focus on reducing delays and achieving permanence for very young children. There is greater awareness of the harmful effects on babies who experience trauma, separation and multiple caregivers. Many local authorities and VAAs are now actively exploring the potential for developing the work. It is recognised that, essentially, concurrent planning is about good child-centred social work practice.

- **Appendices** provide relevant tools and information. These have been provided by Brighton and Hove City Council, Coram and Cambridgeshire County Council. They include: data about the outcomes of concurrent planning by Coram in London and by Brighton and Hove City Council; information leaflets for prospective concurrent carers and for parents; a proforma for a contact agreement; and a practice flow chart.

Included throughout the text are quotes from birth parents and concurrent carers; many of the latter have now adopted. Those who have adopted are described as concurrency adopters. Relevant permissions have been sought and names have been changed.

The implementation of concurrent planning has been patchy in the past. Now, there is considerable emphasis on it and an expectation that local authorities will undertake such planning and facilitate suitable placements, often with the involvement of VAAs. Such work has already started. This guide therefore aims to assist practitioners and managers to put concurrent planning into practice.

2
Research overview

The re-emphasis on the role of concurrent planning has been influenced significantly by research into a number of key areas affecting children. This includes extensive research exploring the impact of early environment and, in particular, the relational world of attachment on the brain development of infants and young children. It also includes studies into the developmental harm that some children experience pre-birth as a result of their mothers' alcohol and substance misuse and/or exposure to violence. The harm experienced through long-term maltreatment after birth has also been extensively explored.

More recently, studies have been undertaken into agencies' responses to maltreatment of children and interventions with families. These studies explore how decisions are made as to whether children should remain with or be separated from their families. They also provide messages about the impact of those decisions, particularly in relation to the likelihood of reoccurrence of maltreatment in a significant number of cases where rehabilitation has occurred.

Studies into the experiences of infants during contact visits while in foster care (including concurrent placements) are beginning to provide a framework for making better quality, child-centred contact arrangements. Research into adoption outcomes provides a clear message that the younger the child is when adopted, the better the chances of good psycho-social outcomes for them. All of this research underpins the role that concurrent planning can play in optimising the healthy development of babies and young children who need foster care and possible adoption. Long-term adoption support will also continue to be necessary for some children and families.

This chapter highlights the main headlines from research and associated theory. (For fuller overviews, see Schofield and Beek, 2006, Ward *et al*, 2012, and Davies and Ward, 2011.) Specific research relevant to practice is also highlighted in individual chapters of the guide. Evaluation and research relating to the operation of concurrent projects to date in the US and England are covered in Chapter 3.

EARLY ENVIRONMENT, ATTACHMENT AND BRAIN DEVELOPMENT

The importance of a child's environment and attachment to their primary caregivers in their very early months and years cannot be overestimated. It is clear that early experiences of relationships and social environment profoundly affect children's development, particularly in the first three years. Extensive research evidence supports this (see overview by Howe, 2009 and Ward *et al*, 2012)

In the first months and years, the child's brain is developing at a phenomenal rate. Through interaction with the social environment and the development of attachment relationships and influenced by genetic factors, the infant and young child is learning about their own thoughts, feelings, perceptions and behaviours and those of others (Howe, 2009). She or he is developing the ability to regulate stress through responses to her or his needs by primary caregivers. If these interactions are reliable and responsive, the child will develop a secure base and internalise confidence in the person to whom they can safely turn when unfamiliar experiences are encountered. It seems clear that the more these experiences are available, the more neuronal connections are made and the richer brain development becomes (Barlow and Underdown, 2008; Gerhardt, 2004).

The **quality** of attachments and environment are of primary importance. Howe (2009) notes:

> *Secure, good enough environments encourage rich, dense, integrated brain development.*

Glaser comments on the importance of the intense and secure bond formed with the primary caregiver (DfE, 2012d):

> *Formation and maintenance of secure attachments protect the developing brain from the harmful effects of stress. Secure attachments happen when the caregiver has spent sufficient time with the infant to be able to "read" and respond appropriately to the infant's non-verbal cues, achieved through stability and continuity of care.*

Perry (2008) (quoted by Humphreys and Kiraly, 2011) states:

> *There are critical periods during which bonding experiences **must be present** for the brain systems responsible for attachment to develop normally. These critical periods appear to be in the first year of life, and are related to the capacity of the infant and the caregiver to develop a positive interactive relationship.*

It is quite clear therefore that secure attachments and a positive early environment provide the optimal conditions for rich brain development (unless adversely affected by organic or genetic impairments). This in turn sets the scene for positive perceptual, social, educational and psychological development.

The impact of insecure attachment and poor early environments on infants' and young children's brain development is equally powerful. Howe (2009) comments:

> ...abusive, neglectful and traumatic caregiving environments can have profoundly adverse impacts on early brain development, the growing nervous and hormonal systems, and the brain's ability to regulate itself.

Ward *et al* (2012) comment that research into the subsequent development of globally deprived Romanian children, adopted into the UK from institutions, showed that parts of the infant's brain can fail to develop without the intense relationship needed with adult caregivers (Chugani *et al*, 2001; Gerhardt, 2004). Without warm and active engagement, key components of the brain are simply not stimulated and thus unable to make the necessary neural connections.

Furthermore, as Ward *et al* (2012) point out, infants whose needs are ignored or rejected by adult caregivers experience high levels of stress. Prolonged and repeated stress affects brain development and activates trauma responses, including the repeated release of cortisol. Over time, there can be a lowering of the threshold for arousal or an over-sensitised stress response (in some cases developing before birth (Wand *et al*, 2001)). For some, there can be abnormally low levels of cortisol, where young children have learnt how to switch off the stress response. High and low cortisol levels have been shown to be linked with a range of psychological and physiological difficulties in childhood and adulthood and are implicated in poor affect regulation (Gerhardt, 2004).

However, as Howe (2009) notes, the brain is often described as "plastic" so that, although early environment and attachment relationships are critical, neurological development can continue to progress. This is particularly the case in the context of close, intense and long-lasting relationships. He comments:

> Improved brain organisation and functioning can...continue in the context of any close relationship, including the relationship abused and neglected children have when they are placed with emotionally attuned and psychologically responsive foster carers and adopters.

Nevertheless, children *placed in infancy* with emotionally attuned carers are more likely to make positive progress than older later-placed children whose internalised working patterns become more difficult to shift (Hodges *et al*, 2003).

PRE-BIRTH EXPERIENCE IN UTERO

There is increasing knowledge about the effects of damaging experiences on the developing foetus in the womb. This may involve exposure to alcohol and/or substance misuse, often exacerbated by poor nutrition (Hill and Edwards, 2009). There may also be transmission of blood-borne viruses, or exposure to violence, feelings of ambivalence, rejection or grief in the mother or maternal illness (Mather, 2004). All of these experiences can have a profound impact on early and future development.

Mather (2004) comments that a child's health and development may be compromised by the exposure to alcohol and/or drug misuse at every stage from conception. For some, the effect can be foetal death or stillbirth. Some babies are born with foetal alcohol spectrum disorder (FASD) and physical features may mean an early diagnosis can be made. Others will be born with potential foetal alcohol effects (FAE) that will affect their development but are likely to only become most evident when they are at school. Some infants will be withdrawing from drugs taken by their mothers in pregnancy. For these children, there may be growth retardation and prematurity (see Phillips, 2004, for a full overview of the impact of alcohol and drug misuse).

Mather (2004) states that:

> Not all children prenatally exposed to drugs and alcohol will have long-term problems; some appear to have minimal or no apparent problems while others have very severe problems and there is a spectrum of difficulties between these two extremes.

Whatever the outcome, babies who have experienced such adversity in utero are very vulnerable. Some may show difficulties in forming attachments even with optimal parenting. Some babies are very sensitive to touch, or may feel overwhelmed in situations where there is a lot of noise and movement (Plant, 2004). These babies need gentle, consistent care with warm and nurturing caregivers who are able to meet their needs and provide the conditions that can optimise their development as far as possible after birth.

IMPACT OF MALTREATMENT ON INFANTS AFTER BIRTH

Howe (2009) provides a very helpful overview of the impact of all forms of maltreatment on children. What seems clear is that the younger the child and the longer time she or he is exposed to maltreatment, the more significant the impact on her or his development and sense of self. Such maltreatment may be occurring during critical periods of brain development when the baby has not yet built much resilience. Abuse can be particularly damaging for infants because the perpetrator is often the very caregiver on whom the infant is depending for safety and comfort.

Ward *et al* (2012) outline that all forms of abuse are harmful and comment that research has shown that up to 80 per cent of children brought up in abusive and chaotic households have disorganised attachments (Van IJzendoorn *et al*, 1999). These disorganised attachments will in turn affect the child's ability to relate to others, their development of empathy and a range of other psychological difficulties. Neglect and emotional abuse can lead to difficulties across all aspects of children's development and may result in 'life-long damage' (Davies and Ward, 2011).

INTERVENTIONS AND RESPONSES TO MALTREATMENT

A number of research studies into safeguarding children across services in England have recently been undertaken. These followed the tragic deaths of Victoria Climbié in 2002 and of Peter Connelly in 2007, both of whom died following long-term abuse and neglect and were known to many agencies. The research studies that followed provide important messages about responses and interventions by agencies when children are at risk (see Davies and Ward, 2011, for a full summary).

Several studies demonstrate that parents who maltreat their children are often dealing with mental health difficulties, substance and alcohol misuse and domestic violence. These difficulties may be compounded by parental learning disability, poor support networks and financial and housing problems. Jones (1998) lists a similar range of difficulties. The researchers conclude that it is crucial to identify difficulties and intervene early and proactively, given the negative long-term impact of abuse and neglect on children's development. They comment that it is vital to intervene early for babies and young children but they also emphasise the impact on adolescents. They also note the particular vulnerability of disabled children.

Several studies provide evidence that programmes that prevent maltreatment are more effective than interventions focusing on the consequences. Targeted parenting programmes can be particularly effective in reducing maltreatment. Nevertheless, there is evidence that the reoccurrence of maltreatment is high (around 50 per cent) following reunification (Farmer and Lutman, 2012). Therefore, there needs to be careful assessment and evidence of sustained and sustainable change prior to reunion. The researchers comment that well-managed and inclusive planning is necessary where parents are provided with focused support to make required changes. This should be done within the child's identified developmental timescale, with clear consequences for parents who do not keep to agreements. They highlight that services will be needed that support families as required, and this may be needed on a long-term basis.

A number of studies demonstrate that 'outcomes for children tend to be better where there is evidence of careful assessment, thoughtful planning and proactive case management' (Davies and Ward, 2011). This is particularly the case for those children subject to child protection plans or care orders. However, the researchers found practice between and within authorities was highly variable. They also found evidence that many children are left too long or returned prematurely to abusive or neglectful families. A number of reasons are suggested for this, including: insufficient knowledge and understanding of child development and the impact of abuse and neglect; desensitisation to evidence of neglect; and the expectation that children will do best if brought up by their birth families (an expectation that can be reflected in the court system where parents are given numerous chances to show they are able to care for their children).

The timing of decision making, particularly for very young children, is emphasised by all of these studies. Concern is expressed that if very young children are left too long in abusive or neglectful families, pending a decision to separate them, their long-term wellbeing may be compromised. The studies suggest tentatively that the parents who are more likely to be able to change and care for their children are: less likely to have been abused themselves; more likely to have come to terms with the removal of an older child; more likely to have support from their extended family and friends; and able to use support from intensive parenting programmes. Ward *et al* (2012), in their study of 57 infants and young children who were identified as suffering or likely to suffer significant harm, made some important findings. In particular, they found that the parents who were likely to be able to care safely for their infants had made substantial changes within six months of the baby's birth and that they had already been making major changes prior to birth. Further exploration is needed for the applicability of these findings to larger groups of children.

SEPARATION, CONTACT AND TRANSITIONS

Davies and Ward (2011) comment:

The evidence suggests that maltreated children, and particularly those who are neglected or emotionally abused, may benefit by being looked after away from home. Where there has been evidence of past abuse, and particularly neglect, maltreated children who remain looked after find greater stability and achieve better wellbeing than those who return home.

Many babies and young children who are at risk of significant harm are removed from their birth parents and birth family's care and some are eventually adopted. However, the practice of how and when separation occurs and permanent placements are made can have a profound effect on those babies and young children. Ward *et al* (2012), in their study of infants, found that 35 per cent were permanently separated from their birth parents. Of those infants, 60 per cent experienced late separation from their birth family followed by the disruption of a close attachment with a short-term foster carer when they were moved to their permanent family. They noted that courts often did not reach final decisions for many months whilst further assessments were undertaken and more expert reports were requested.

In the meantime, infants and young children experienced intense, sometimes highly distressing and often very frequent contact arrangements with their birth family (Humphreys and Kiraly, 2011; Kenrick, 2009; Schofield and Simmonds, 2011).

Kenrick (2009) undertook a retrospective study of 26 concurrent carers, now adopters, from Coram's concurrency planning project. The former concurrent carers interviewed were all involved in the contact arrangements and transported children to and from the contact centre, an arrangement that contrasts with that of young children in temporary foster care where the foster carers are often not involved in the transport arrangements. The narratives of these concurrency adopters provide compelling accounts of infants and carers' experiences. Features included: the difficulties caused by lengthy journeys to and from contact; constant disruption to routines for vulnerable children; and the impact of almost daily contact over several months. This was particularly difficult when babies had reached the developmental stage of separation anxiety between five–eight months of age.

Humphreys and Kiraly (2011) undertook a larger study in Australia of the experiences of contact for infants under one year of age in foster care (not concurrent placements), and their findings were very similar. They commented on the poor quality of much of the contact and concluded that there was no correlation between the rate of reunifications and frequency of contact: it was the quality of contact that was of most importance. They highlighted concerns about the numbers of different supervisors involved and the impact on infants and young children who were often transported to contact by strangers. They commented on the importance and complexity of both maintaining the infant's relationship with their parents, whilst also enabling the infant to settle into a predictable routine with a highly attuned carer.

Schofield and Simmonds (2011) emphasise that vulnerable infants need opportunities through skilled and attuned care to recover and develop. They comment that infants' positive development and a secure base provided by good foster care will aid either successful reunification or adoption.

As Ward *et al* (2012) note, most infants and young children who are separated from their birth families are placed in at least one temporary foster care placement for the duration of proceedings. They are later moved to an adoptive family once the court has agreed that they should be adopted. This means that an already very vulnerable young child has to manage further significant disruptions to her or his attachment relationship(s). Even with the best foster care placement and the best adoptive family, the move from foster carer to prospective adopter will be difficult and sometimes damaging.

Often for very young children, this transition to an adoptive family occurs a year or more after entry into care. For some children, this transition can occur after a significantly longer period in care during which they are likely to have become settled with their carers.

EARLY PLACEMENT FOR ADOPTION

Van den Dries and colleagues (2009) found that babies who are placed early for adoption are more likely to form secure attachments to new carers. The rate of disruption for very young children is low (Biehal *et al*, 2010). In Biehal *et al's* study regarding outcomes of different placement options, they found that for children adopted before their first birthday, the disruption figure was about two or three per cent.

Simmonds (2009) outlines messages from a review of a range of adoption studies by Juffer and van Ijzendoorn in 2005 and 2007. Juffer and van Ijzendoorn (2005) conclude that 'adoption is a successful intervention that leads to remarkable catch-up in all domains of child development'. They found this to be particularly the case for infants who were removed early from adverse and/or abusive environments. Simmonds notes, however, that 'many UK children adopted from care will be older at removal and at placement and will have suffered a range of abusive and/or neglectful experiences'.

Argent and Coleman's guide *Dealing with Disruption* (2012) provides a useful overview of disruption studies to date. The authors note that 'broadly speaking, disruption studies of children *placed after infancy* confirm an average rate of 20 per cent, with a range of 10–50 per cent'. Clearly therefore, for older children, the risk of disruption is much higher and disruptions usually occur as a result of high levels of emotional, behavioural and relationship difficulties (Rushton and Dance, 2004).

Selwyn *et al* (2006) focused on 130 children aged between 3 and 11 years when a plan for adoption was made between 1991 and 1996 in England. The average age of these children when they came to the attention of services was six months. They experienced serious adversity and significant delays before entering long-term care, and further drift occurred in care planning. By the time of the plan for adoption, they found that many of the children were displaying significant emotional and behavioural difficulties and some older children were never placed for adoption. The odds of not being adopted increased by 1.8 for every year of the child's age.

Ward *et al* (2012) conclude from a range of research findings:

> *There are strong indications that the younger the child is when placed for adoption, the better the chances of both a stable placement and successful psychosocial outcomes. The older children are at placement, the more likely they are to display behavioural problems, including problems with peer relationships, attachment, conduct disorder and poor concentration (Biehal et al, 2010, Haugaard et al, 1999), and therefore the greater the risk of disruption.*

Further research across England into disruption rates and reasons behind them has been commissioned by the Department for Education. It is expected that the results of this research will be available in late 2013.

IMPLICATIONS OF THE RESEARCH FINDINGS

As stated, the research into the development and needs of babies and very young children is extensive. Much of it has relevance to concurrent planning and supports its use for vulnerable infants and young children who are at risk of significant harm. We know that secure attachments and good enough environments provide the best conditions for infant growth and development, with the first three years being critical. There is also evidence that proactive assessments and timely interventions can lead to "good enough" parenting by parents. There is also evidence to show that parents who sustain changes and care successfully for their infants have generally made significant changes before the child's birth and within the first six months of the child's life.

There are times where there is the need to separate infants from their families whilst focused work is undertaken. There may be a chance of rehabilitation and this needs proactive engagement and focused intervention with families. This work needs to be undertaken within the infant's timescales for security and permanence, and is aided by good quality contact arrangements.

Concurrent planning can support these objectives very effectively. However, it will not negate the need for good quality long-term adoption support when required for particular children and families.

3
History of concurrent planning

INTRODUCTION

The term "concurrent planning" was originally used and developed in the US in the early 1980s by the Washington State Department of Social Services through its work with Linda Katz at Lutheran Social Services of Washington and Idaho. It was developed in response to concerns about the damage of drift and delay in effective planning for children in the care system. At that time, in common with child care planning in the UK, there was a sequential approach to permanence planning.

This sequential approach focused on the primacy of family reunification but the consequences of this were that children remained in temporary foster care for years, with many experiencing multiple moves. Concurrent planning works to reduce the consequences of this damaging process for vulnerable children in the care system and provides the opportunity for a child to be placed with carers able to offer the security and stability of a permanent home through adoption, if that child cannot be safely placed within their birth family in a timely way. As stated in Chapter 1, concurrent planning literature often refers to Plan A – the plan to work towards rehabilitation of the child in foster care, whilst at the same time being prepared to implement Plan B – the adoption of the child by the foster carers with whom the child is placed.

The model of concurrent planning developed in the US was used by the innovators of this approach in England who worked to adapt the model to make it compliant with the English legislative framework, while adhering to the basic principles of the US scheme. Many of the messages from the US experience are of particular relevance to teams in the UK that are considering developing concurrent planning as a care planning model in appropriate circumstances for infants in the care system.

HISTORY OF CONCURRENT PLANNING IN THE US

In 1996, Linda Katz wrote about the first 15 years' experience of running concurrent planning schemes. The care system in the US was at that time overwhelmed by very young, neglected, drug-affected children with a poor prognosis for successful rehabilitation. She saw concurrent planning as an effective care planning model for these vulnerable infants. In her experience, there were particular benefits in looking at the existing barriers that were in place to linking foster carers, adopters and birth families in the best interests of children. Concurrent planning ensured a more open approach to permanency planning, with its dual plans and the importance of contact for children with their birth parents. She acknowledged that ethical questions had been raised about the scheme and doubts expressed about how much support was given to birth families to enable them to work to resume the care of their children. She also dealt with the fact that there were low numbers of children who returned to birth families.

In her view, this resulted from the children coming from families where the prognosis for rehabilitation was very poor from the outset, given the significant issues of concern within their birth families. As in the UK, the court required very clear evidence of the assessment of the birth parents and their engagement with support services in order to decide that adoption was the right care plan. She said:

> The foster carers are exactly that and receive no special consideration since the entire legal case centres on the birth parent's fitness or unfitness.

(Katz, 1996a)

The fundamental principle underlying child welfare policy in the US is that children are better off if they can be brought up by their birth parents. This preference for the role of birth parents is codified in law and provides the rationale for retaining reunification as a core outcome for children placed in foster care. Concurrent planning promotes the notion of "success redefined", with the goal of early permanence for the child, with family reunification as the first but not the only option. Intrinsic to the model is the belief that adults, rather than children, should take on the emotional risk of foster care.

> Concurrent planning assumes that adults are better able to manage the ambiguity of relationships and the uncertainty of an unknown future than are children – so, the emotional burden is shifted.

(Northern California Training Academy, 2009)

Since the early US development of concurrent planning in the 1980s, there was patchy implementation of the model elsewhere. The Adoption and Safe Families Act of 1997 paved the way for greater use of concurrent planning as it permitted, although did not require, concurrent planning as a process that child welfare agencies could use to expedite permanency planning. The use of concurrent planning steadily grew. A study in 2005 found that 87 per cent of child welfare agencies in the US had implemented some form of concurrent planning (Mitchell *et al*, 2005).

Lutheran Community Services undertook an in-depth piece of evaluation work in 2003. They reviewed the records of children who were placed concurrently between 1981 and 1998 and followed this up with an adoptive parent survey and interviews with adoptive parents, birth parents, young adopted adults and professional stakeholders. The report concludes that:

> *Based on this evaluation of concurrent planning at Lutheran Community Services, timely permanence generally leads to long-lasting stability, relationship permanence and improved wellbeing for children in foster care.*

Of 169 children who were placed from 1981–1998, 89 per cent were adopted, nine per cent were reunified with birth parents and two per cent had a different outcome such as guardianship by extended family. Most of the children who were placed came from birth families where there had been significant substance misuse issues.

The report showed that one in six adoptive parents returned to the agency for additional child placements. The report states that:

> *As a group, these permanency planning parents displayed dedication to the children in their care, despite feeling that concurrent planning pushed them to the limits of their coping abilities.*

Significantly, adoption support services were identified as an important resource for these families. The follow-up study with 83 families post-adoption found that 76 per cent had utilised mental health services and 63 per cent specialist educational support services. Adopters reported that the teenage years had been most challenging, but 93 per cent of children and young adults who were adopted through the programme experienced permanence and were currently living at home or transitioning to independence.

(Northwest Resource Center for Children and Families, 2003)

In her 1999 article, Linda Katz described the benefits and pitfalls of implementing concurrent planning, which have significant lessons for teams within the UK. She highlights in particular:

- the need to guard against equating concurrent planning with adoption and minimising reunification efforts;

- the problems caused by failing to accommodate cultural differences and the need for staff to be culturally competent as in other areas of work with families;

- the need for goal-orientated casework and for effective practice to work to support the parents' engagement with services;

- the need for collaboration with other adult treatment providers, recognising that mental health and substance misuse treatment services have a different clientele than child welfare services and there can be conflict over goals and timescales. The development of multidisciplinary collaboration is important to avoid conflict;

- the need for workers to have effective training and to be competent within the court arena;

- the need to avoid giving concurrency carers an evaluation of the level of risk involved when a child is placed with them;

- the importance of carers accepting that there is no guarantee as to the outcome apart from the role they will be playing in providing the least detrimental experience for the child;

- the need to provide effective training and ongoing support to concurrency carers to equip them for the challenges of the task.

Katz states that:

Child welfare's responsibility to provide services to parents must be fulfilled in good faith or we violate both ethical and legal standards. Concurrent planning is not mere window dressing for expedited adoption. If it becomes that, it will have sacrificed all integrity.

She concludes that:

...a well run concurrent planning program can minimise the enduring psychological harm caused to children by multiple placements and years in the limbo of out-of-home care. Although such efforts may not be a "miracle", they are an improvement that is sorely needed and worth our best efforts.

(Katz, 1999)

THE CURRENT SITUATION IN THE US

A report was published in April 2012 by the Child Welfare Information Gateway, part of the Children's Bureau in the US, on the evidence relating to the concurrent planning model. The Child and Family Service Reviews, which all States are required to produce, were considered in relation to their reference to concurrent planning. All 52 States indicated that concurrent planning was being implemented to varying degrees. However, there were a number of difficulties being cited with implementation, including staff not having a clear enough understanding of the concurrent planning model and a need for a programme of ongoing additional training. In some States, there was also resistance to the model from courts and attorneys.

This report also acknowledged that there were few published studies providing a comprehensive evidence base for the practice, with most consisting of tracking outcomes and gaining qualitative information from key stakeholders. However, despite these caveats, the report stated that there was evidence of children achieving permanence more quickly. There was also evidence of the effect of a more open approach and direct communication between parents and carers, which had resulted in more parents accepting a plan for adoption and more "open adoptions" involving some form of ongoing contact post-adoption.

The Child Welfare Information Gateway report (2012) outlined system characteristics that 'appear necessary, in combination for the full functioning of a system of concurrent planning'. These essential elements are of particular relevance to agencies within the UK considering implementation of concurrent planning. These are:

- agency support at all levels for the principles, priorities and practices of concurrent planning;

- institutionalisation of the approach through the use of formal systems for resolution of paternity issues and relative search, documented reunification prognosis-tracked timelines and procedures for referral between workers and regular review meetings;

- support for caseworkers which included formal and informal training, shared decision making and manageable caseloads;

- integration of child welfare and adoption units working towards the same concurrent goals;

- an adequate pool of concurrent carers who are willing and able to work towards both reunification and adoption;

- services available to support birth parents to work towards achieving reunification goals;

- support from judges, attorneys and other court personnel for concurrent planning philosophy and practice.

A number of studies also profiled the skill needed by caseworkers to work effectively with parents regarding both Plan A and Plan B and the potential tensions inherent in that role.

> *It is important that both caseworkers and their supervisors accept the philosophy of concurrent planning and believe that it is possible to work in good faith with parents while at the same time planning for an alternative permanency goal.*

(Child Welfare Information Gateway, 2012)

D'Andrade *et al* (2006) found that concurrent planning was often well-developed and understood by adoption staff but was poorly understood by front-line staff, with caseworkers falling back on to sequential planning. The role of supervisors was highlighted, as they require the skills and time to involve themselves closely in timely case planning and decision making. Frame *et al* (2006) suggested the potential for integrating child welfare and adoption staff organisationally and structurally to facilitate ongoing communication and collaborative goal setting.

HISTORY OF CONCURRENT PLANNING IN ENGLAND

There was initially little certainty about how the US experience would translate into UK practice. However, the premise for concurrent planning fitted with the concerns emerging in the early 1990s about delays and drift for children in care, multiple placements and limited success of some of the family support and family breakdown prevention schemes. The emphasis in the Children Act 1989 on partnership working with families had in many situations limited early statutory intervention in families where children may have been suffering chronic neglect. The longer-term damage to young children associated with extensive periods in the care system was beginning to be widely recognised, along with the impact of late placement for adoption. There was also a greater understanding within social work of attachment theory and early child development.

The Quality Protects programme was introduced by the Department of Health in 1998 to address some of these problems, and had as its first objective 'to ensure that children are securely attached to carers capable of providing safe and effective care for the duration of their childhood' – which clearly fitted with the objectives of concurrent planning.

Three specialist concurrent planning teams were set up in England in the late 1990s. The Goodman team was instigated as a part of the Manchester Adoption Society (MAS) in 1998 and undertook much of the pioneering work through the links established by their then Director, Brian Clatworthy, and the concurrent planning team in Seattle.

The Goodman team needed a lengthy planning period, networking with key agencies in the area and the local judiciary to gain agreed sign-up for the model. They initially worked with two local authorities in the area – Bury and Salford – and took over responsibility for undertaking the parenting assessment and provision of contact arrangements for children who were placed with their carers. As a VAA, key worker responsibility for the child remained with the local authority social worker.

The specialist team within Coram, another VAA based in central London, was set up in 1999. It was modelled on the Goodman team, although Coram decided that they would focus on children aged under two, whereas Goodman had initially set up their team more in line with the US model and potentially offered placements to children up to the age of eight years. Coram worked initially with two local authorities in London – Camden and Islington.

At the same time as Coram became established, the first local authority specialist team was set up in Brighton and Hove. This team was established following a local multi-agency conference on early permanence planning which had the US pioneer Linda Katz as a keynote speaker. This event proved to be a catalyst and the opportunity for funding came through the Quality Protects grant. The team ran as a small fieldwork unit and was based and managed within the Adoption and Permanence team. Brighton and Hove recruited social workers with experience of care proceedings and of parenting assessments and inducted them in fostering and adoption practice.

There was very close liaison between the teams at the time and Margaret Adcock acted as a specialist social work consultant to all three teams.

Initial development work

Initially, the teams worked to familiarise themselves with the model, produce literature about the scheme for prospective carers, birth parents and professionals and establish protocols within their agencies for referrals. Liaison with a range of different professionals and other agencies including social work teams, health staff and adult substance misuse and mental health workers, Children's Guardians and the local judiciary was undertaken and steering groups established in each area. A lead-in time of at least 12 months was required after staff were in post before carers were approved who could be considered for children with a concurrent care plan.

It was a feature of all the teams that there were lead professionals who were very supportive of the model and played a key role in promoting the scheme. Within Brighton and Hove, for example, the senior lawyer sat on the steering group, assisted with developing a court protocol for transfer of cases with a concurrent care plan to the county court, ensured her staff team were fully briefed on the model and acted as a liaison with the local legal community to enable time for concurrent planning to be profiled on the local Family Justice Group agenda. Similarly, the medical adviser within Brighton and Hove, who had regularly contributed to the preparation group training, endeavoured to make herself available to meet prospective concurrent carers when a match was being considered, given that these infants were often only a few days or weeks old at the time of placement.

The collaboration between the pioneering teams assisted in the development of recruitment and assessment tools. An early concurrency adopter from Goodman helpfully attended the first preparation groups in Coram and Brighton and Hove to share her firsthand experience and reflections on the model.

Parenting advice and support work

All the teams were small, with a specific staff member who had responsibility for supervision of contact and provision of parenting support and advice. The teams endeavoured to work to the model established in Seattle which highlighted, in particular, the support available to birth families in the early stages of placement and the very proactive approach to seeking out wider family members who could play a role and avoid any drift in the planning. Parents who did not arrive for an assessment or contact appointment were followed up straight away and reminded of the very short timescale for the work, given the needs of their baby.

The US workbooks profiled three stages for the work with birth parents: 'doing for, doing with and cheering on'. All the teams used this model in their practice and provided a range of support services in the early stages of the work. This included assisting parents with practical issues like welfare benefits or housing difficulties, and working to ensure that the parents received a responsive and proactive social work service. The teams all experienced some parents remaining in touch after a care plan for adoption had been agreed and provided some time-limited ongoing support work.

Social work roles

For each child placed with concurrent carers, there was a separate allocation of a social worker to undertake the assessment with the parents and a supervising social worker for the carer. It was essential that these roles remained separate, although good communication between the workers, including the worker undertaking the supervision of contact, was crucial. Social workers undertook different roles in each particular case so they gained an understanding from both viewpoints.

As the Brighton and Hove team was based in the local authority, casework responsibility was transferred at the point that the concurrent care plan was agreed in court. However, the team members worked very closely with fieldwork colleagues to undertake pre-birth assessments. If a care plan for concurrency was agreed in court, the plan for further assessment built on the work already undertaken during the pre-birth stage. The team's involvement in pre-birth assessments enabled proactive work to consider any potential wider family and friends carers and resulted in a number of recommendations about care plans other than concurrency, e.g. a placement with parents with a support plan, a placement within the wider family or a parent and baby foster placement.

The focus on early identification of potential referrals was very important for all the concurrency teams.

'An emotional roller coaster'

There were teething problems for all the teams and Goodman and Coram had to work to maintain a high profile in their areas to ensure that referring social workers from the local authority were aware of the model. This was less of an issue within the local authority team in Brighton and Hove, as the team was directly involved in undertaking pre-birth assessment work and had opportunity for early consideration of potential referrals.

Whilst many concurrent carers reflect on their experiences during the concurrency process as an 'emotional roller-coaster', this phrase can also be used to describe the experiences of the teams. From initial teething problems, there were many highs and lows during the first 10 years of practice in the UK, with emotions often running high about the efficacy of the model, given the fact that very few babies were rehabilitated, or that the primary focus was on young babies who were easier to place for adoption, rather than older children or sibling groups.

There were also many debates about the role and frequency of contact. All the teams experienced having to work with a care plan that involved much higher levels of contact than they had recommended. The teams stressed that parents' involvement in contact was very important in terms of maintaining their bond with their child and providing an opportunity for focused parenting skills work, as appropriate. However, for all the families with children placed concurrently, there were significant issues that needed addressing outside of the contact arrangements.

In 2004, Kent County Council set up a dedicated team based in the Thanet area managed within the adoption service. Goodman and Coram also extended their operation by accepting referrals from a wider range of authorities.

Many other local authorities considered the option of developing a concurrency team but did not pursue this. Whilst there was often widespread recognition of the potential value of such a way of working, there were reservations about the capacity to undertake the work to set up a dedicated team and the length of time and commitment needed before such a team could be fully operational. However, there have been pockets of concurrent planning practice being used by some local authorities for a small number of infants where adoption is a very high possibility at the outset of proceedings.

Another factor that hindered the development of further specialist teams was the experience within the court setting, where at times there was considerable opposition to a concurrent care plan, in part because of the very high adoption rate of children placed concurrently being associated with a "back door route to adoption". There was also a limited "window of opportunity" to consider a move to concurrent carers during the process of care proceedings. In a number of situations, Children's Guardians or others opposed a move to concurrent carers if the infant had already started to settle in a placement with mainstream foster carers.

All of the teams considered children for concurrent placements if the potential for adoption as an outcome was high from the information that was known from the assessment of the parents and background history prior to placement. In reality, for many of the placements made, adoption was a very likely outcome if the issues of concern were of a very longstanding and chronic nature. There were only a very small number of children successfully rehabilitated to birth parents or wider family. By 2009, there had been 147 children placed by the then four concurrent planning teams in England. Of those, eight returned to their birth family, with two of those subsequently coming back into care.

The low rehabilitation rate in concurrent planning should be seen in the context of rehabilitation rates for all young children subject to care proceedings. Ward et al reported on a study in 2006 where they tracked 42 babies in the care system. They showed that very young children whose mothers had entrenched alcohol and/or drug problems were very unlikely to be reunited with them. In this cohort of children, only one returned home on a permanent basis.

Research by Farmer in 2009 has also shown that there is a very high failure rate in relation to children who were rehabilitated from care proceedings; 47 per cent of those children who returned home were back in care within two years.

Evaluation work undertaken by Monck *et al* (2003)

An independent evaluation study was built into the planning for the Goodman team. The evaluation was undertaken by Monck *et al*, based at the Thomas Coram Research Unit, and expanded to incorporate the work of the three pioneering teams. They tracked the outcomes for the children placed with the teams and provided information from interviews conducted with carers, birth parents and staff involved with the projects.

In 2003, their evaluative report gave an overview of practice issues and concluded that there were speedier resolutions of permanence plans for children placed concurrently and that these children experienced fewer moves than other adopted children. The researchers compared the speed of placement of concurrency cases with children younger than 12 months across the whole of England who were taken into care and for whom adoption was the outcome. They found that there was an average of 26 months in care for the national sample, double the time taken on concurrency cases. The evaluation study also commented that despite early doubts, all the teams had been able to successfully recruit prospective concurrency carers.

As a result of their early evaluation work, Monck *et al* concluded in 2003 that 'it is possible to say with confidence that concurrent planning worked well for the children in the study'.

There was a small follow-up piece of evaluation conducted by the original research team which reported in 2006 (Wigfall *et al*). It specifically focused on the experience of practitioners and managers from Brighton and Hove and London authorities linked to the Coram team. These interviews indicated that there was still some confusion about the model, with a few practitioners remaining unclear about the difference between concurrent planning and twin-tracking or parallel planning. There were also difficulties reported with Guardians or lawyers being doubtful or sceptical about the concurrency model and opposing such care plans in court.

This report also highlighted the fact that there had been an uneven flow of referrals to the teams and at times difficulty in taking on referrals if carers were not available who fitted the child's matching criteria. Reasons for the teams not being able to take on some referrals included the ethnicity of the child, the location of the birth family and proximity to available carers and the child being part of a sibling group. The opportunity for carers and birth parents to meet and develop some form of relationship was generally seen as positive, and the evaluation found that significantly negative relationships between the birth parents and the carers was the exception.

Wigfall *et al* (2006) concluded that:

> ...*evidence from this evaluation indicates that concurrent planning can be a valid approach in a small number of selected cases, but it is certainly not an easy project to implement.*

THE CURRENT SITUATION IN THE UK

England

The first concurrency team, Goodman, ceased operation in 2010 when the Manchester Adoption Society was forced to close due to financial difficulties. The specialist team within Brighton and Hove closed in 2009, in part due to the decreasing number of concurrency cases being agreed in court at the time and a significant rise in the use of parent and child fostering resources, particularly for babies where the local authority initiated care proceedings at birth. The financial constraints within local authorities also added to the pressure to reduce spending on smaller specialist teams. Brighton and Hove, however, remained very committed to the model and has continued to recruit carers and to place a number of babies concurrently in recent years. Brighton and Hove has also continued to share their experience and expertise in operating concurrent planning within a local authority and moving to "mainstream" the model. See Chapter 8 for more information on models of delivery.

The specialist team in Kent closed in 2010, having faced very similar issues to those experienced by Brighton and Hove. The capacity of a small scheme in Devon that was set up in 2006 was affected by the loss of a lead adoption manager, although Devon has retained a commitment to the model.

Due to the Government agenda on early permanence, a large number of local authorities and voluntary adoption agencies across the UK are currently considering the possibility of developing concurrent planning. Coram in London has maintained a specialist team and is being funded by the Government to become a National Centre of Excellence in Early Permanence. Coram has been tasked to support the development and implementation of the concurrent planning and fostering to adopt models.

There have been pockets of activity on concurrent planning throughout the country with different authorities and some voluntary adoption agencies working to develop their capacity to provide such a placement for at least a few very young babies subject to care proceedings where adoption is a clear potential outcome.

Scotland

There has been some interest in considering the lessons from the experience of the England concurrent planning teams within Scotland. In 2011, the Scottish Children's Reporter Administration produced a report highlighting delays in decision making about permanence (including for babies) and the often multiple moves for the small percentage of children in the care system who are adopted. The Scottish Government Response to this report, also published in 2011, promised further work to look at ways of reducing delay and ensuring key messages and research on attachment and child development, including early brain development, were incorporated into new policy and guidance.

A number of local authorities on the east and west coasts of Scotland are currently exploring the potential for developing concurrency projects with the support of CELCIS (the Centre of Excellence for Looked After Children in Scotland). A Concurrency Planning Implementation Partnership has now been set up in the east, working in partnership with voluntary adoption agencies. Ongoing development work is also underway with local authorities on the west coast.

Northern Ireland

There is some experience of concurrent planning in Northern Ireland. In 2007, Kelly *et al* reported on a scheme run by the Northern Health Trust which focused on improving processes of permanence planning for children in care. This scheme involved recruiting "dual-approved" carers – essentially prospective adopters who were "stretched" to undertake the fostering role for children whilst assessments were being undertaken with their birth parents. Placements were made where the prognosis for rehabilitation was poor. Carers were successfully recruited and the children placed with these carers had fewer moves and a more settled path to permanence via adoption. The children placed were not just infants, although 50 per cent were aged under two and 17 per cent were over five years. This model focused on the recruitment of appropriate carers and did not involve the establishment of a specialist concurrency team that also undertook the dedicated assessment service to birth families. A number of Heath and Social Care Trusts in Northern Ireland have continued to recruit these concurrent carers and place children with them on a fostering basis. Kelly *et al* reported that these carers need good preparation for the task and a high level of support to sustain them through the often stressful fostering phase.

In 2009, the Family Care Society, a voluntary adoption agency, was granted three-year project funding from the Department of Health and Personal Social Services in Northern Ireland to establish a concurrent planning service. This team (called Unite) is the only specialist concurrent planning project in Northern Ireland and provides an assessment service to birth families as well as the recruitment, support and supervision of concurrency carers. The team has made use of consultation and advice from experienced concurrent planning practitioners in England. A small staff team were appointed in 2010 and the first placements made in August 2011. The Unite team also describes a lengthy setting-up process, which involved establishing a stakeholder group and networking with all the appropriate agencies, including the local judiciary and other legal professionals.

SUMMARY OF LESSONS FROM THE PIONEERING UK TEAMS

- There is a need for adequate "lead-in" time when plans are being made to establish the model.

- Key stakeholders need to be identified and an ongoing programme of training and familiarisation with the model will need to be planned. The potential for a local stakeholder group should be explored, particularly within the development phase.

- Responsibility for championing the model and overseeing the development and operational practice should be held by a small number of key strategic managers.

- Methods for collecting data on numbers and profiles of babies and infants subject to care proceedings need to be put in place so that information can be gathered on the potential cohort for this model.

- Processes need to be developed for early identification of potential referrals.

- Recruitment of carers is possible but time is needed to raise the profile of the model within recruitment material and at publicity events. The use of information from experienced carers can be very helpful and additional time is needed to ensure all aspects of the concurrency task are covered within the preparation training and considered fully during the home study assessment. Assessing social workers, key managers, panel members and agency decision makers need to be fully briefed.

- An intensity of support to carers is essential, along with good communication between the workers for the child and the supervising social worker for the carers.

- There are different models of operating concurrent planning and there has been a gradual evolution within the UK from the specialist team model that endeavoured to adhere closely to the US model. It is helpful to understand the history of the programme within the US and the experiences of the teams within the UK. There is significant merit in considering the potential for enabling some infants to have the opportunity of early placement with a concurrency carer, even if the assessment of birth parents is undertaken through the more traditional means within the local authority. Implementation issues are discussed more fully in Chapter 8.

4

The legal framework

CONCURRENT PLANNING: BASIC LEGAL PRINCIPLES

When stripped away to its essentials, the legal underpinning of a concurrent placement is extremely simple. Where the court confers on the local authority the power to place a child in foster care, it is open to the authority to place the child with approved foster carers who are also approved as suitable to adopt. As a matter of law, the child is first placed with the carers selected by the authority in their capacity as foster carers. The status in law of the carers will change from foster carers to prospective adopters, and the status of the placement will change from a foster placement to that of adoptive placement, **only if:**

- a final care plan for adoption is approved by the court;

- a placement order is made; and

- the local authority approves the match between the foster carers and the child in their capacity as prospective adopters.

Thus during the care proceedings, and prior to any placement order being made, **there is literally no difference whatsoever in law between the status and legal obligations to a child and their birth family where the child is placed with foster carers via concurrent planning, and where a child is placed into mainstream foster care.**

Prior to the making of a final care order, the child's status and the considerations of the court in respect of interim care planning are no different from any other child placed in the interim care of the local authority, either via powers under s20 Children Act 1989 or s38 Children Act 1989.

Concurrent placements are not to be confused with "twin tracking" or "parallel planning". These phrases are used where the search for long-term alternative carers takes place in parallel with assessments of the family within care proceedings while the child is placed with foster carers. In this form of planning, if the court determines that the child will not return home, the child will leave their foster placement and move to prospective adopters. However, under concurrent planning the child will not have to make such a move. Concurrent planning focuses solely on whether or not the child can return to live with their family, and if not, the child will be adopted by their foster carers.

The national profile of concurrency may be greater now, but concurrency is not a new concept. The High Court recognised the value of a concurrency scheme in the last century. *In Re D and K (Care plan: twin track planning)* (1999) 2 FLR 872, Mrs Justice Bracewell encouraged local authorities to establish concurrency projects in England and Wales. She said:

> *The aim is to reduce the number of moves a child experiences in care, and to reduce temporary placements. The project involves the recruitment of foster parents who are carefully selected and trained and who are willing to foster children on the basis that they will work with the natural family towards rehabilitation within a strictly timed framework but in the event of rehabilitation being ruled out, wish to adopt the children. Contact between carers and birth parents is encouraged and there is openness between the parties about the primary aim of rehabilitation with the alternative secondary plan of permanent placement. Placement stability is a top priority.*

Whilst the legal basis upon which a local authority can choose to place a child with carers who are approved both as foster carers and adopters is not complex, the potential areas of challenge to this form of interim care plan need to be understood and addressed from the outset. They need to be treated with respect and met head on.

There is nothing in concurrent planning, per se, which promotes injustice for the child or their family, or does not fit within the principles of the Children Act 1989. In fact, concurrent planning can be said to bring real meaning to the child's welfare being paramount within proceedings. There is much in concurrent planning which is entirely congruent with the transformation agenda of the Family Justice Review and pending reforms of the family justice system. It shifts much of the stress and uncertainty about future placements from the child to the adults. It provides protection for the child against the impact of delay.

There is also nothing inherent in concurrent planning which reduces the prospect of parents resuming the care of their child or, where this fails, reduces the prospect of them having an ongoing relationship with the child post-adoption by concurrent carers. Experience from the specialist teams that operated within England suggests that, when it works, it can offer an enhanced model for parents even where their children go on to be adopted by the concurrent carers they first knew as the foster carer for their child.

Those seeking to place children via a properly managed concurrency scheme therefore have nothing to fear from the issues addressed below. They must be capable of providing the reassurance needed by the courts and parties to proceedings to demonstrate that concurrency is entirely congruent with justice for the child.

The starting point for a concurrent placement is achieving the legal authority to place the child with foster carers in the first place. Where parents are not consenting to a foster placement under s20 of the Children Act 1989, the court must be persuaded that there are grounds for an interim care order. It must also be persuaded that a care plan which envisages the removal of the child from their parents into foster care is in the interests of their welfare and is proportionate and justified under the applicable legal test for removal. The foster carers selected must be approved and suitable for the task. There is nothing about the concurrency scheme which dilutes these first principles.

PRE-PROCEEDINGS – ADHERENCE TO THE PRE-PROCEEDINGS PATHWAY OF THE PUBLIC LAW OUTLINE AND APPROPRIATE APPROVAL OF THE POTENTIAL CARERS

Expectations under the Public Law Outline: formulating the interim care plan

The authors of this chapter heartily endorse the sentiment expressed in Chapter 1:

> *Concurrent planning must take place in the context of proactive care planning and court proceedings where birth parents are fully represented.*

The key elements underpinning concurrent planning apply long before the case reaches court. For a decision to be taken to issue care proceedings, to seek the removal of a child and a placement in foster care, the allocated social worker must have conducted an assessment of the parents. They must have concluded that removal into care is proportionate to the evaluated risk to the child and that there is a likelihood of a plan for adoption being the preferred outcome if the parents cannot address the issues identified in the child's timescale. Pre-proceedings assessment (including pre-birth where applicable) and adherence to the elements of the Public Law Outline are essential. The need for skilled pre-proceedings assessment will become all the more important once the amendments to the Children Act are introduced which require the court to timetable towards care proceedings being concluded within 26 weeks, wherever it is just to do so.

Where there has been inadequate assessment prior to the issue of proceedings, the prospect of the court approving any local authority care plan is diminished, particularly if the authority is seeking the most draconian interim step of removal of the child into care. Chapter 5 makes specific recommendations in respect of the timing and nature of the assessments required. It is essential that cases which need a pre-birth assessment are identified at the earliest opportunity. The assessment will need to be conducted proactively and early enough in the pregnancy for it to properly inform post-birth care planning.

Where local authorities have concluded that a child will be the subject of care proceedings, and the recommendation to the court should be one of removal into care, local authorities are required to have due regard to their obligations under Adoption Statutory Guidance 2011. As stated in Chapter 1, local authorities are currently required to consider concurrent planning:

> *Concurrent planning is usually most appropriate when the child is under two...It is not the right option for all children, for example, those who are already in a stable foster placement but for whom adoption subsequently becomes their plan, or where the need for care is to be short-term, and older children. But it should always be considered, in the context of care planning as a whole, as one of the possible options for achieving permanence for a child.*

It is also essential for the local authority to recognise that one of the options for achieving permanence will always be that a child is cared for by their wider family. Thus in considering whether a concurrent interim care plan will be the optimum plan for the child, the local authority **must** have due regard to their obligation to assess the family. Chapter 5 contains further detail about practice and the relevant statutory guidance regarding these assessments.

It is important to note that if there is a family member who may be able to provide an appropriate safe and nurturing home for the child, even if only in the short term, then concurrent planning would not be appropriate.

Approval of concurrent carers

If asked, most lawyers will accept that concurrency is theoretically a child-focused way to conduct care planning for some of the most vulnerable children in society. However, many lawyers are sceptical whether it is possible to find carers who can genuinely accept and be committed to a dual fostering and adoption role. Concerns have been raised that this is "adoption by the back door". The reality is that experience has shown it is possible to recruit concurrent carers, but it is essential that it is done properly. In *D & K* ([1999] 2 FLR 872):

> *Not every case will be suitable for such placement. Generally it is likely to apply to babies or young children where there are some but by no means optimistic prospects in relation to rehabilitation to the natural*

family. Only a selection of cases will come within the ambit of such a scheme. The experience is that such foster parents can be recruited and the outcome for children has proved beneficial.

Statute already envisages the opportunity for a child to remain permanently in a foster placement, not just by the mechanism of long-term care but also by recognising that foster carers fall into a special class if they seek to adopt in their own right under the Adoption and Children Act 2002.* We can think of many cases where the child has been placed with foster carers for the duration of the proceedings and the Children's Guardian and judge will ask, 'Is there any prospect of the foster carers being prepared to offer long-term care?'

In contrast to the unplanned evolution of a foster placement into a prospective adoptive placement, a concurrent placement has the advantage of transparency. The parents are aware of this possibility from the moment the child is placed. A concurrent placement gives the opportunity to ensure that this is a plan of choice, and that relationships with the parents develop accordingly, not as a default position.

Historically, concerns have been expressed that there is a potential conflict of interest where the local authority or agency has approved the concurrent carers, and recommended that a child be placed with them with a possibility of adoption, as well as making recommendations to the court about whether or not the child should be rehabilitated to the parent's care. This is another concern which can be addressed through a comparison between a concurrently placed child and a child placed in a mainstream foster placement. In law, there is no difference between the decisions facing the court and the law that the court must apply, or the local authority's duty to the child's family, irrespective of whether a child is placed in foster care with mainstream foster carers, or in foster care with concurrent carers. The key factor is that the child is not being placed with the carer as an adopter, but in their capacity as a foster carer. There are national minimum standards for fostering which concurrent carers must be assessed as meeting. However, it must also be acknowledged that this type of fostering comes with additional challenges, and the capacity to meet those challenges must be incorporated into rigorous assessment and approval regimes of the approving agency. The additional requirements of concurrent carers, which are set out in Chapter 6, should offer some reassurance to those who may be concerned that it is not possible to find carers able to manage the added complexity of the role.

---

* Where a child has been in a foster placement for one year, the foster carers do not need the permission of the local authority to apply to adopt the child, but can make an application in their own right under section 42(4) Adoption and Children Act 2002.

Perhaps the key difference from mainstream fostering is the level of uncertainty that the concurrent carers will have to manage. Prior to approval, the assessing social worker needs to evidence the applicants' capacity to manage a sustained period of uncertainty and the potential, or actual, loss of the child if rehabilitation becomes the plan. For birth parents to have confidence that the concurrent carers will genuinely work towards rehabilitation, the agency which has approved the carers will need to be able to demonstrate that their assessment has properly tested the concurrent carers' understanding and acceptance of the following points:

- their role as foster carers;

- that there is no room for social engineering in care proceedings;

- that the primary objective of the care proceedings is for the child to be raised within the birth family, if they can provide good enough care; and

- that work is being undertaken to pursue rehabilitation actively with the birth parents or wider birth family.

In short, the selection and training of concurrent carers must be demonstrably aligned to the Government's view that:

> ...the carers must be well-trained and be able to cope emotionally and practically with the possibility that they may not go on to adopt the child in their care.

(Department for Education, 2012c)

Approved concurrency carers must also understand that during the care proceedings parental responsibility rests with the parents and the local authority. Key interim arrangements for the child will be the subject of an interim care plan which will require the approval of the court.

The plan of concurrency should not drive any element of the care plan to be considered by the court, apart from choice of placement. The driver for any plan of assessment, services and contact to be offered to the child's birth family will be what is in the child's best interests (the paramountcy principle), and what is necessary to achieve the right outcome for the child within the parameters of the law. Those approved as concurrent carers will need to be able to manage the level of disempowerment this may cause them to feel. It is recommended that preparation groups for potential concurrent carers should include an element of training on the legal framework within which concurrent carers will be required to care for any child placed with them. This will ensure an understanding of the legal constraints upon them as carers, and the limits of the placing authority's powers within care proceedings.

The other key difference between mainstream foster carers and concurrent carers is the degree to which the concurrent carers will be expected to be involved with contact handovers and develop a relationship with the birth parents, where safe to do so. The level of interaction between concurrent carers and the parents of the child can be much higher than via a traditional fostering route. The Statutory Guidance refers to the carers' role in relation to contact:

> *This involves placing a looked after child with approved foster carers who, as well as providing temporary care for the child, bring them to regular supervised contact sessions with their parents and other relatives. In addition, the carer spends time with the parents at both ends of contact sessions to update them on the child's progress. This enables a relationship to develop which is supportive to the parents.*

Where this is successful, it can potentially add immense value to the ongoing relationship between the concurrency carers and the birth parents post-proceedings, whatever the outcome of the care proceedings.

The earliest point at which the carers have a right to make decisions about the child is if the child is ultimately made the subject of a placement order, **and** the local authority decides to change the status of the placement from a fostering to an adoptive placement. Once a placement order is made, the Adoption and Children Act 2002 enables the local authority to make a placement for adoption. It also enables them to determine the extent to which parental responsibility can be exercised by the local authority, the birth parents and the prospective adopters with whom the child is placed for adoption (s25(3), Adoption and Children Act 2002). Therefore, until such time as the adoption order is made, the prospective adopters (as they will now be in law) share parental responsibility.

Matching

The concurrent carers will have been approved by the local authority or a VAA as both foster carers and prospective adopters. This will have involved the carers being considered by the local authority or relevant VAA adoption and permanence panel, a recommendation being made to the agency decision maker (ADM) and a decision made to approve them as foster carers and prospective adopters. They will then be carefully matched with a child as concurrent carers under fostering regulations (see Chapter 5).

There is no capacity under the current regulatory framework for the adoption panel to make an *in principle* approval of an adoptive match between the concurrent carer and the child prior to the concurrent (foster) placement being made. No such match can be made until a plan of adoption has been decided upon by the local authority. (This guide recommends that such matches are considered after the court has granted a placement order). Since the adoption agencies regulations were amended in September 2012, the decision as to whether or not a child's best interests are served by a plan for adoption rests solely with the local authority's ADM. Any subsequent match between the concurrent carers and the child as an adoptive placement must first be the subject of consideration by the relevant local authority's adoption and permanence panel, before a recommendation is made to the ADM and a final decision made. This guide identifies the need for local authorities to develop careful protocols around the matching process prior to placement with the concurrent carers.

The local authority has a responsibility to the child and to the concurrent carers to ensure there is full disclosure of relevant background information concerning the child. The duties of local authorities to both foster carers and adopters in this regard is well established, with potential consequences in litigation if these are breached. Again, the notion that this duty arises because of the concurrent status of the foster carers can be overstated. As the National Fostering Minimum Standards 2011 state:

> *Prior to the placement of each child, the foster carer is provided with all the information held by the fostering service that they need to carry out their role effectively. The information is provided in a clear, comprehensive written form and includes the support that will be available to the carer.*

The prospective concurrent carers need to be clearly advised that the information in relation to the child they are considering is confidential.

THE APPLICATION TO THE COURT – IS REMOVAL INTO CARE JUSTIFIED, IS AN ORDER NEEDED?

Once the decision has been made that a concurrent care plan is the preferred option for the child, unless the child is a relinquished baby, the local authority will issue its application for an interim care order. As the formulation of the concurrent care plan requires planning and pre-assessment, we suggest that an application for an emergency protection order is not the correct route if it can be avoided.

Where the case is to be issued upon the birth of a child, the local authority should be ready with its application for an interim care order. The maternity unit at the hospital should be invited to keep the mother and baby together on the ward if at all possible until the court is able to fix a hearing of an interim care order application. CAFCASS should be notified that this is the plan and placed on notice of the likely due date, and alerted when the mother goes into labour. The court should be advised of the need for a hearing as soon as the baby is born. Where possible, an agreement should be reached with the parents (having had the benefit of legal advice) that the baby will stay on the ward until the court determines the outcome of the first hearing.

An application to remove a child from the parents and place the child with concurrent carers should be no different to an application to place the child with ordinary foster carers. If the court is satisfied that the child's physical or emotional safety requires immediate separation, then the interim care order should be made *if* the court approves the terms of the interim care plan.

It is theoretically possible to place a child with concurrent carers under s20 of the Children Act 1989, but we do not recommend this, as s20 placements are reliant on the consent of the parents and are inherently uncertain. The ethos of concurrency is to reduce the number of changes of placements for young children in care and to promote the forming of secure attachments, which should only be broken if the court assesses that the birth parents are able to provide long-term good enough care. The local authority has no power to prevent the removal of a child from a s20 placement and urgent applications would be required if consent were to be withdrawn. If the case has been carefully assessed and the facts of the case justify removal, it is our view that the need for the local authority to share parental responsibility is usually evident.

It may be that agreement to s20 accommodation is raised at court in opposition to the making of an order, it being said that no order is necessary if the parents fully support the plan. The social work statement to the court will need to provide an analysis of the reasons why the needs of the child require that the local authority shares parental responsibility. This must be an analysis of the risks in the case and an indication that for the full benefits of a concurrent placement to be available for the child, these should not be jeopardised by a reliance on consent.

When hearing an application for an interim care order, the first issue for the court to determine is whether the threshold criteria pursuant to s31(2) Children Act 1989 are satisfied, as modified by s38(2) Children Act 1989. Section 31(2) provides that a court may only make a care order or a supervision order if it is satisfied: (a) that the child concerned is suffering or is likely to suffer significant harm; and (b) that the harm or likelihood of harm is attributable to (1) the care given to the children or likely to be given to him if the order were not made, not being what it would be reasonable to expect a parent to give him, or (2) the child being beyond parental control. Section 38(2) modifies this test so that, for an interim order, the court must be satisfied that there are 'reasonable grounds to believe' that the s31(2) criteria are met.

If satisfied that the threshold criteria are met, the court will then go on to consider the welfare checklist under s1(3) Children Act 1989 to determine what order, if any, is required to protect the welfare of the child. As part of that assessment, the court will also consider Article 8 (right to private and family life) of the European Convention on Human Rights (ECHR). It will only make an order where the interference is provided for in domestic law, the interference pursues a legitimate aim, is necessary in a democratic society and is a proportionate response to the protection issues in the case, the legitimate aim being to protect the "health and morals" of the child.

A considerable body of case law has developed concerning how the court should approach the application to separate parent from child. In the case of *Re H (A Child) (Interim Care Order)* (2003) 1 FCR 350, the Court of Appeal considered the interplay between the welfare of the child and the Article 6 (right to a fair trial) and Article 8 ECHR rights of the parents. The court stated that the parents' ECHR rights:

> *...required the judge to abstain from premature determination of their case for the future beyond the final fixture, unless the welfare of the child demanded it. In effect, since removal from these lifelong parents to foster parents would be deeply traumatic for the child, and of course open to further upset should the parents' case ultimately succeed, that separation was only to be contemplated* **if the child's safety demanded immediate separation**. *(at [39])*

Since the decision in *Re H*, the definition of harm within s31(9) Children Act 1989 has been amended to include 'impairment suffered from seeing or hearing the ill-treatment of another' in addition to 'ill treatment or the impairment of health'. Development is defined as 'physical, intellectual, emotional, social or behavioural development'. 'Significant' is defined as 'considerable, noteworthy or important' (see Children Act 1989 Guidance 1991 at paragraph 3.19 and *Humberside County Council –v- B* (1993) 1 FLR 257).

In *Re A (Children) (Care proceedings: threshold criteria)* (2009) EWCA Civ 853, when expressing a meaning of "significant" harm, Ward LJ stated:

> *...the harm must, in my judgment, be significant enough to justify the intervention of the State and disturb the autonomy of the parents to bring up their children by themselves in the way they choose. It must be significant enough to enable the court to make a care order or a supervision order if the welfare of the child demands it.*

In *Re R (a minor)* (2009) EWCA Civ 942, Wilson LJ states that "likely" is defined as meaning a real possibility that could not sensibly be ignored having regard to the nature and gravity of the feared harm in the particular case.

Thus a plan of concurrency can only be developed where the legal test for the removal of a child into foster care is likely to be met. This is the ultimate safeguard for the parents against a fear of social engineering, or "adoption by the back door". *Re H* made it clear that in the balancing act carried out by the court, when deciding whether to approve a care plan for removal, it will only be necessary and proportionate to interfere with the child's and parents' Article 6 and 8 ECHR rights by approving separation if the welfare of the child "demanded" it. Thorpe LJ stated that separation needed to be 'essential to secure the child's safety' (at [40]). This principle has been restated in subsequent authorities (see *Re M (Interim Care Order: Removal)* (2006) a FLR 1043; *Re K and H* (2007) 1 FLR 2047; and in *Re L-A (Children)* (2009) EWCA Civ 822).

It is important for the court to be reminded that the concept of safety referred to above includes psychological and emotional safety (see *Re B* (2010) 1 FLR 1211). The decision whether the separation of parent and child is in the child's interests, at an interim stage of the proceedings, is a question with respect to the upbringing of a child to which section 1 of the Children Act applies. The court's paramount consideration is the welfare of the child (see *A Local Authority v KAB* (2010) 3 FCR 1). In *Re L (A child)* (2013) EWCA Civ 489, Black LJ stated that 'the focus of an interim care hearing is upon what may happen to the child during the interim period if he or she continues to live with or returns to live with his or her parents. An interim care hearing is not designed for the purpose of evaluating the longer-term future except insofar as that is necessary to give directions for the management of the case'. The social work statement to the court should address the safety issues, both physical and emotional, that require the child to be separated from the parents and why separation should not, for the welfare of the child, wait until the final hearing. It should not concentrate on what the predicted outcome of the proceedings is thought to be, even though that prediction may have led to the authority's decision to pursue concurrency in the case.

UNDERSTANDING AND ADDRESSING PERCEPTIONS AND CONCERNS ABOUT THE INTERIM CARE PLAN

Where the test for the removal of a child has been met, the court must go on to consider the interim care plan. Those presenting concurrent care plans to the courts need to have a very clear understanding of the legal principles involved and the arguments that are likely to be raised by those parents and advocates who oppose this model of foster placement. The statement drafted by the social worker should aim to address these.

Approving the interim care plan

The terms of the concurrency care plan should not in our view be very different, if at all, from the interim care plans presented in all removal cases. Our experience of concurrency cases has been that the apparently low incidence of children being returned to their birth families (noting that the nature of the comparators for this analysis are not always clear), the structure of the work with the parents and child and a perception of an inflexible approach to contact arrangements have led some legal practitioners to view concurrency placements with suspicion, and even hostility. Where they cannot persuade the court that the placement of the child into care is unnecessary, the only means to challenge the concurrent placement will be an attempt to challenge the elements of the interim care plan. The challenges are likely to focus on three areas, although in theory only one of those areas relates to the key distinguishing feature of concurrent planning:

Challenge to the choice of foster placement, being a carer with dual approval as an adopter

Providing the court with a very clear presentation on the law and highlighting the division of responsibility between the court and the local authority under the Children Act 1989 is, in our view, the essential first step in any concurrency application. What is different about an application for the approval of a concurrency care plan is the plan for the foster carers to adopt the child if a full care order and placement order is made at the conclusion of the care proceedings. Can the court refuse to approve an interim care plan on this basis? The case of *Re L (Interim care order: power of court)* (1996) 2 FLR 724 sets out the jurisdiction of the court when considering interim care plans.

> *In my judgment the position is this: first, an interim care order is a holding order which should not be treated as an indication of how the matter will be finally disposed of. No irreversible decision has yet been made as this mother fears. Secondly, an interim care order is none the less a form of care order. Section 31(11) says so because a care order is there defined to include an interim care order made under s38. Accordingly, once made, the care of the child passes to the local authority and the manner in which the child is cared for passes out of the control of the court. It must follow that the court has no more power to impose conditions on an interim order than it has to give directions under a full order.*
>
> *All of that, however, is subject to s38(6). That does give the court a power to intervene and to give such directions as it considers appropriate with regard to medical or psychiatric examinations or other assessments of the child.*

Thus the court has the power to order assessment under s38(6) Children Act 1989 when making an interim care order, but that is the limit of its jurisdiction. **In short, the court cannot direct the local authority in how to care for the child, or where the child is to be cared for, unless it refuses to make the interim care order and makes supervision or residence orders.**

In the *Matter of M (a child)* (2009) EWCA Civ 1486, the Court of Appeal was asked to consider a case where it was plain an interim care order was necessary, but the Children's Guardian and mother did not agree to the local authority's proposal to move the child to different foster carers. An appeal was dismissed by a circuit judge who decided that he was 'powerless to intervene' because this was not a case where it was better for the child for no order to be made. The circuit judge also pointed out that the only avenue of legal challenge open to the mother was to claim judicial review of the local authority's care plan on the basis that it contravened the principles of public law. The case then came before the Court of Appeal, which refused to grant the mother permission to bring a further appeal. In making its decision, the Court of Appeal observed that the courts below had not had 'any real choice' in how they dealt with the choice of placement by the local authority where the grounds for an interim order were made out:

> This point immediately raises a dilemma which has exercised the judiciary ever since the Children Act was implemented. Prior to the implementation of the 1989 Act, Parliament had left the power to dictate where a child should live with the court. The court could direct the local authority to place the child in a particular placement and the court retained control over the local authority's action. All that was changed by the 1989 Act, and in the well known case of A v Liverpool City Council (1982) AC 363 the House of Lords decided authoritatively that once a care order had been made, whether final or interim, the court was effectively faced with a choice and not a choice which was in any sense attractive. It could either make a care order whether or not it agreed with the care plan, or it could decline to make a care order. If it declined to make a care order then the child would not be subject to any form of intervention subject to the ongoing proceedings but would return to the care of her mother in this case. If the court made an interim care order the child would be subject to the local authority's interim care plan.

This reconfirms that where the court decides that a child should be the subject of an interim care order, it has no power to decide where a child is to live under the interim care order. Any challenge to the local authority's decision making was to be by way of judicial review. The authors note that the proposed amendments to the Children Act 1989 under the Children and Families Bill 2013 envisage that at final order stage the areas of the final care plan the court may have regard to will be specifically limited to that of placement, and contact arrangements under s34(11). *

---

*   Children and Families Bill s15 care plans:

(1) For section 31(3A) of the Children Act 1989 (no care order to be made until the court has considered section 31A care plan) substitute—

(3A) A court deciding whether to make a care order—

(a) is required to consider the permanence provisions of the section 31A plan for the child concerned, but

(b) is not required to consider the remainder of the section 31A plan, subject to section 34(11).

What the court can do is to indicate those parts of the interim care plan with which it does not agree, and invite the local authority to amend those provisions. The Court of Appeal has said this on many occasions, and this was emphasised in *Re S and W (Children) (Care proceedings: care plan)* (2007) 1 FCR 721. It was said that there should be co-operation between the court and local authorities and that the local authority should be open to changing its care plan if that is what is requested. That said, the local authority cannot be forced to change its care plan and local authorities are often very resistant to doing so. The court would then be faced with the choice between making the order on the basis of the local authority's care plan, or making some other, or no order.

This issue was considered by a circuit judge in Brighton in 2006. The case involved the local authority's proposal to place a baby with concurrent carers, there having been recent care proceedings that resulted in the older children being removed and placed for adoption. The interim care plan for concurrency was opposed, not on the basis that the child was to be placed with concurrent carers, but on an objection by the Children's Guardian that the specific concurrent carers selected by the authority were a same-sex couple. The legal arguments concerning whether the court or the local authority had the responsibility for deciding on the foster carers was fully argued before the circuit judge and is of relevance irrespective of the sexuality of the concurrent carers. The circuit judge ruled that the assessment and selection of foster carers was a matter entirely for the local authority and not for the court. The judgment in this case was expressly endorsed by Sir Mark Potter, the President of the Family Division at the time, in a speech he gave to the British Association for the Study and Prevention of Child Abuse and Neglect in the summer of 2006 (reported at [2006] Fam Law 1036).

Given the clarity of the law in respect of the choice of placement, we would encourage those establishing concurrency schemes not to enter into agreements with local courts that require a separate or special approval of a concurrent care plan. The law the court must apply is no different from any other interim care plan. The selection of the foster carers is quite simply a matter for the local authority.

For the court to give an indication that concurrency was not an appropriate model for any child, we suggest that there would need to be some extremely compelling factor in the case. Assuming that the local authority has been successful in addressing the other practical arrangements in the care plan so that there is no sustainable argument that the parents "got less" in a concurrency case than they would get in a non-concurrency case, and given the clear advantage to the child of not having to move placements if having to be placed outside of the family, it is difficult to think of a reason why any court would wish to interfere with the local authority's exercise of its duties in selecting a placement most advantageous to the child. In considering any question regarding the child, the focus of the court at all times must be on the welfare of the child. The court must also have regard to the child's timetable.

Those seeking approval of a concurrent care plan will need to be able to explain how the plan offers advantages to the welfare of the child. Where adoption is a real possibility, if the child's parents cannot make the changes expected of them, the advantages to the child of avoiding a move to another carer are, in our view, common sense. In addition, they are now underpinned by a research base which is hard to challenge (see Chapter 2). Practitioners recommending or considering a concurrent care plan should familiarise themselves with, and be prepared to use, this research to support their own evidence to the court that the child's welfare is best promoted by the approval of the concurrent care plan. Confident use of the research will assist in developing the understanding of the court, and the parents, that concurrent planning can optimise the healthy development of babies and young children who need foster care and possibly adoption.

Whereas the court is unable to dictate the choice of foster placement, it does have powers in relation to the assessment of the family, and the contact arrangements.

Challenge to the care plan in respect of the programme of assessment of the parents, or effective assessment of parents – ensuring a level playing field

(i) Entry criteria

In our experience, challenges raised about the "entry criteria" for a concurrent care plan are a red herring; however, this does not prevent them being raised. Local authorities that introduce concurrent planning schemes may find, initially at least, that a forensic attitude is taken as to whether or not the case merits the referral to a concurrency placement. The problem with this approach is not that it cannot be properly addressed, but that it adds so little to the real issues with which the court must be concerned.

A plan for concurrency should only be considered by the local authority where there is:

> ...clear evidence of sufficient concern about the parents' circumstances to warrant not just issuing care proceedings but also a plan for separation, with adoption as a potential outcome if changes cannot be made within the child's timeframe.

We advise against using criteria which can be too easily redacted into percentages, which can then be argued about in court. By setting overly rigid or precise "entry criteria" for concurrency placements, the local authority is seen to be pre-judging the outcome of the proceedings by deciding at the start that the parents have a low or very low chance of keeping their children with them. Lawyers representing parents see the decision to restrict concurrent planning to those children most unlikely to be returned to the parents as prioritising the needs of the concurrency carers over the needs of the parents. The arguments raised are that concurrency schemes do not want to place children with concurrent carers if those children have a good chance of returning home, as a return home would be too difficult for the carers to cope with if their true desire is to have their own child through adoption rather than providing a service by fostering. If there was a real chance of a child returning to the parents, then recruiting concurrent carers would be extremely difficult.

(ii) Assessment of the parents' capacity to resume care of the child

In our view, the notion that by placing adoption as a possibility up front in the proceedings the local authority is being unfair to parents or skewing the assessments that follow does not bear scrutiny. Such an argument undermines the crucial need for transparency in the relationship between the local authority social worker, the parents and the court. Parents need to know that any worker involved in care planning will be open and honest with them. The pre-proceedings element of the PLO is of course predicated on the notion of the "wake up call" via the letter and meeting before action. In cases that involve young children and which the court considers so serious that it approves the removal of the children, it is obvious that the authority will be *required* to consider adoption as an option if it concludes that the child cannot safely be returned home. Where adoption is under consideration, the local authority is also required to make parents aware of this possibility and offer information under the Adoption Agencies Regulations and Adoption Statutory Guidance:

> The possibility of adoption will not arise suddenly and unexpectedly; in many cases during the early stages of the local authority's involvement there will be a need for "twin-track" or parallel planning, including concurrent planning. In any case where there is a possibility that adoption may become the plan, it is incumbent on the local authority to ensure that the parents are aware of this possibility and provided with information about its significance, and information about the support available. Thus some of the duties laid out in AAR 14 (counselling and information for parents) will have been carried out before the review at which adoption is identified as the plan for the child.

(Adoption Statutory Guidance)

The difference with concurrency is that, where it is safe to do so, parents have the opportunity to develop a relationship with the potential adopters of their child prior to any decision for adoption having been made. They can therefore see for themselves the level of commitment this carer is willing to make. Where an atmosphere of trust can be established, the opportunity for the parents to develop an enhanced relationship is actually likely to be to their advantage if the court decides the child cannot return to their care and sanctions a plan of adoption.

At that stage, the relationship between the parents and prospective adopters will be highly significant when the court comes to consider arrangements for any contact with the child post-adoption. The real experiences of parents expressed in Chapter 5 should offer some comfort in this regard.

The reality is that most parents have some insight into their own difficulties, even if they do not express it during the course of the care proceedings, and most parents want the best for their children. Their capacity to see that concurrency may offer the best for their child, if they are not successful in maintaining care, should not be underestimated.

Local authorities may be faced with opposition at court to the concurrent care plan unless those representing the parents are convinced that there is no disadvantage to the parents by agreeing to such a plan. If not, the interim care order application may be opposed on the basis that the case has been identified as suitable for concurrency, whereas the interim care order would not be opposed if the plan was to place the child with non-concurrency foster carers. For those promoting the interests of the child, such arguments will be viewed as completely missing the point of concurrency and not promoting the child's best interests. What local authorities have to appreciate is that those representing parents have to put their interpretation of "best interests" on the basis of the client's instructions. If it is thought that agreeing to concurrency is more likely to lead to a full care order and adoption than agreeing to a standard foster placement, the parents will argue that their child deserves a better chance of returning to the parents so it is, therefore, not in the interests of the child to be placed with concurrent carers.

Maligning the motivation of the child's allocated social worker to work with the parents in a concurrency interim care plan is unhelpful, and in our experience highly unlikely to form the basis of a successful challenge. The model of working and assessment within the Brighton and Hove concurrency project was challenged in the Court of Appeal in the case of *W (A child)* (2004) EWCA Civ 450. Of the challenge to the concurrency model of working, Lord Justice Mantell said:

> *A number of criticisms are made with regard to the way in which the local authority proceeded and the way in which the matter was dealt with by the judge. It seems to me that the matter can be dealt with quite shortly...The criticisms made are threefold: firstly, that the process being operated or the method being adopted by the local authority, which I have referred to as a concurrency plan, is such as to lead to, at the lowest, a possible conflict of interest because the local authority who are charged with seeking to achieve reunification of the family, if at all possible, are concerned with, under what is called the paramountcy principle, to seek a future for the child that is in his best interests. It is argued that these two objectives can produce a conflict of interest. I fail to see how that attack can be properly supported, provided always that*

those charged with securing the objectives act throughout in good faith and recognise that the primary purpose of their work is, if at all possible, to keep the family together. If, however, that is incapable of achievement, then of course the overriding principle that they must act in the best interests of the child takes over and that must be secured by the best possible means available.

Lord Justice Mantell went on to say the judge found:

...having heard evidence, that those charged with carrying through the programme acted in good faith and accordingly rejected the complaint being made as to the nature of the programme itself. To my mind there is nothing in that proposed ground of appeal. It would be doomed to failure.

These are clear words from the Court of Appeal that there is no conflict of interest for a social worker within a concurrency team being responsible for assessing the parents while also being responsible for securing the adoption of the child, if the parents are ultimately found to be incapable of providing good enough care. It is our view that the challenge put on behalf of the parents could also have been put to any social worker in any care proceedings that result in a recommendation for adoption. The allocated social worker in all proceedings has this dual role – assessing the child and securing permanence if the child cannot return home. This decision serves as a further demonstration of how concurrency cases are, from a legal perspective, no different to any other case. It is not in the interests of the concurrent care planning team to seek to present it as anything other than a form of foster care that is more advantageous to the child. Neither is it in their interests to suggest that special treatment by the local court is required for concurrency to operate. The ultimate safeguard for the integrity of the proceedings remains the court. The court has no obligations to the concurrent carers or the local authority beyond the obligation of justice to the child.

Much has been made of the low rehabilitation rates of children who have been the subject of concurrent care plans. In our view, this has created something of a vicious circle. The experience of the authorities which have engaged in concurrent planning is that the courts and CAFCASS have leaned towards approving concurrent interim care plans for very young children where there is a very low prospect of rehabilitation at the outset of the case. Any experienced judge or advocate will recognise those cases. On that basis, it is entirely unsurprising that a very low percentage of concurrency cases are successful at achieving rehabilitation: it is, in fact, what was expected from the outset. The small percentages of rehabilitations are then quoted to justify an argument that the scheme must be inherently flawed and skewed towards the needs of the foster carer to retain the child rather than the right of the parent to have their relationship with the child promoted. These arguments can be answered by a fair, transparent and rigorous plan of assessment and services for the parents.

The authors are unaware of any successful challenges to the adoption of children who were placed with concurrent carers. Thus, as there is no evidence that the court's judgment that adoption was the right outcome in law and in fact was flawed, it must follow, for those children who were adopted by their concurrent carers, that the concurrency scheme was entirely to their advantage.

The requirement of 26 weeks for the conclusion of care proceedings and the increased restriction on the use of experts and independent social workers sit well with the concurrency model. Whereas there might have been opposition to concurrency on the basis that the parenting assessment was being undertaken by the social worker allocated within a concurrent planning scheme rather than from an independent social worker, the January 2013 amendment to rule 25.1 of the Family Proceedings Rules 2010 requires that expert or independent social work evidence must be 'necessary to assist the court to resolve the proceedings'. In determining whether an external assessment is necessary, rule 25.5(1)(e) FPR 2010 requires the court to consider 'whether evidence could be given by another person on the matters on which the expert would give evidence'. The model of internal assessment should now pose little difficulty at the interim care order stage. If a detailed assessment is available from the social worker, it will now be much more difficult to oppose a concurrent care plan on the basis that the parents want an independent assessment. If the social worker has completed the pre-birth or pre-proceedings assessment, subject to any expert assessments that are permitted on matters that are outside of the skills of the court, the allocated social worker (if different) or the Children's Guardian, updating the existing assessment to take into account such changes as the 26 week timescale permits, should not be a lengthy exercise and the 26 week timeframe should be readily achievable.

Where an interim care plan has been developed and approved by the court that a parent and child fostering placement or residential resource is appropriate, consideration can be given to concurrency as a contingency plan. Where this is the case, it should appear on the interim care plan so that there is absolute clarity for the parents and their advisers in advance of any residential arrangements being made. This will enable the local authority to place swiftly with concurrent carers in the event that the placement with the parent breaks down and avoid an unnecessary interim placement for the child.

Challenge to the interim contact arrangements, or contact arrangements – a level playing field

Contact plans should be tailored to each child's needs, with research and practice experience informing the assessment of the appropriate contact regime. There needs to be close liaison between the child's social worker, the carer's social worker and local authority lawyer in considering the most appropriate plan. A concurrent interim care plan that only permits contact three times per week will almost certainly be opposed if the local practice at that particular court is for babies to have contact with their parents four or five times per week. There is an increasing practice (based on research set out in Chapter 7) of more restricted parental contact, as taking the child out of the foster placement on five or seven days a week may not be in the best interests of most children.

The usual expectation within concurrency schemes is that the child's concurrent carer will be expected to transport the infant to and from contact. In our view, where achievable, this offers a "gold standard" for contact arrangements. Few of us would wish our children to be transported to contact with any members of our family by people they did not know.

Chapter 7 contains a number of recommendations about the way in which contact should be prepared for and managed, which we readily endorse. We suggest that, were they to be adopted in non-concurrency cases, this would lead to a considerable improvement to the value of the contact regime within proceedings.

THE FINAL CARE PLAN: REHABILITATION TO THE PARENTS OR ADOPTION?

As in any care case, social workers must be alive at all times to the need to consider rehabilitation and the return of the child. The law demands nothing less: in *Re B* (2010) EWCA Civ 324, para 21, Wall LJ held that where the interim threshold is satisfied, the test for *keeping* a child in care at an interim hearing and not returning the child to the parents was stated as being:

> *...whether the continued removal of the child from the care of parents is proportionate to the risk of harm to which she will be exposed if she is allowed to return to the care of her parents.*

Where the authority recommends rehabilitation to the parents, a careful interim care plan will need to be developed which is tailored towards the child being able to successfully achieve a safe rehabilitation in a timescale which meets their needs. The needs of the concurrent carers will, of course, have to be managed by the agency in order that the child is protected from any natural feelings of sadness by the carers that the child will be moving on. It is highly likely that the foster carers will need additional support by their own allocated worker. At this stage, the shift of the emotional burden of uncertainty onto the adults will really come into play. Where parents and the carers have been able to develop a relationship, this is likely to be enormously helpful in the transition period and interim care planning should factor in the recommendations made in Chapter 7.

WHERE THE PLAN IS FOR ADOPTION

Until such time as the court considers and approves the local authority care plan for adoption and a placement order is made by the court, no assumptions can be made and the status of the concurrent carers will remain that of foster carers.

As stated earlier, the placement order cannot be applied for until such time as the ADM agrees that the local authority social work team can put forward a plan of adoption. The ADM should only make that decision if compliant with the recommendations in *Hofstetter v LB Barnet*.*

The court will apply the Act in deciding whether or not the grounds for a placement order have been made out. Here, the basic principles underscoring all decisions in relation to adoption sit well with the aims of concurrency:

- *s1(2): The paramount consideration of the court or adoption agency must be the child's welfare through his life;*

- *s1(3): Delay is likely to prejudice the child's welfare.*

The court will apply the adoption welfare checklist under s1(4); in particular, those aspects which differ from the checklist contained in the Children Act 1989:

(c) the likely effect on the child (throughout his life) of having ceased to be a member of the original family and become an adopted person;

(f) the relationship the child has with relatives and with any other person in relation to whom the court or the agency considers the relationship to be relevant, including:

(i) the likelihood of any such relationship continuing and the value to the child of its doing so;

(ii) the ability and willingness of any of the child's relatives, or of any such person, to provide the child with a secure environment in which the child can develop.

---

*   In *Hofstetter v LB Barnet and IRM* (2009) EWCA 3282 (Admin), the court set out guidance for the way in which the decision maker should approach a case.

All the features of good practice in planning for and supporting adoption apply to concurrency cases, and are detailed elsewhere in this guide.

SUMMARY

Agencies must take seriously concerns that a plan of concurrency may impact adversely on the outcome for a child's parents. Each element of why that fear is held must be dissected and addressed with respect. Where concurrency cases are run to the principles described elsewhere in this guide, there can be real reassurance to parents, their advocates and the Children's Guardian that the process has been implemented in such a way as to ensure at all times that the concurrent care plan offers no disadvantage to the child's family and every advantage to the child.

There are aspects of the concurrency schemes as they have been run which promote positive advantages for parents. The positive reaction of parents to their experiences, even where their child has gone on to be adopted, is testimony that properly run schemes are far from disadvantageous. If concurrency was the "gold standard" for all children under two years of age, many of the arguments raised would fall away.

The ultimate arbiter and safeguard is, of course, the court. The court is not interested in adoption scorecards, and the court's position on social engineering has been perfectly plain for many years. As Dame Elizabeth Butler-Sloss indicated in 1991 in *Re K (Wardship: adoption)* (1991) 1 FLR 57, CA:

> *The question is not, 'Would the child be better off with the Plaintiffs?'*
> *but 'Is the natural family so unsuitable that... the welfare of the child*
> *positively demanded the displacement of the parental right?'*

Concurrent planning is generally appropriate in cases where, in the very early stages of proceedings, displacement of parental rights via adoption is understood to be a realistic possibility should work with the family fail. It is hoped that this chapter shows that the law to be applied when making interim orders, timetabling and care planning is the same as in any other case. The law is blind to the status of the foster carers with whom a child may be placed. It should not be blind to the advantages to the child of enabling the earliest possible secure attachments to be developed at a crucial stage in a child's development. Furthermore, it should not be blind to the advantages of reducing the number of moves for a child before a permanent home can be found either with their parents, or with adopters. In that respect, properly run concurrency schemes can translate the aspiration that the child's welfare should be paramount into practical arrangements for the child's care throughout the proceedings.

5
Concurrent care planning pathway

This chapter explores the care planning pathway, from pre-birth assessment to decision making about a concurrent care plan and matching. Early identification of children for whom a concurrent care plan may be appropriate is essential. Local authorities will need to consider this, where appropriate, as part of the pre-birth assessment pathway.

PRE-BIRTH ASSESSMENTS

Most local authorities have practice guidance on undertaking pre-birth assessments developed through multi-agency discussion and agreement. It is good practice to establish protocols for early referral and the midwifery service is likely to be a key source of such referrals. The booking interview is a time for information gathering and an opportunity for the midwife and the mother to plan the mother's care in pregnancy. It is also an opportunity for the midwife to make an assessment of any specific health and social needs. In some areas, there are specialist midwifery services for drug- and alcohol-using mothers and these often offer a more flexible, informed and responsive service. However, there are many women with whom local authorities become involved who do not access antenatal services at all or in a timely way.

Local authority protocols in relation to pre-birth referrals should cover how and when such referrals are made and how data on potentially vulnerable babies is held and used to safeguard and plan for both mother and baby. It may be helpful for one social work manager to take a lead strategic role in relation to pre-birth assessments to ensure these referrals are given sufficient priority and that active communication with other key agencies is maintained. Many local authorities are now establishing permanence tracking panels, which could expand their remit to include consideration of pre-birth referrals of vulnerable infants who may become subject to care proceedings at birth. Such a focus on a proactive approach from the outset enables the pre-birth period to be used for essential assessment work and for parents to be supported to access appropriate services in a timely way and potentially make the changes necessary to avoid local authority intervention though court proceedings. There are very many demands on busy social work "children in need" teams but developing a capacity to respond quickly to such referrals is critical.

A core assessment will need to be undertaken if it appears that an unborn baby may be at risk of significant harm. Calder advocates pre-birth multidisciplinary assessments commencing by 20 weeks gestation (Calder, 2003). The assessment will focus on the key question of whether the baby will be safe in the parents' care and what prospect there is for the parents being able to care for their child in the future, i.e. what is their parenting capacity? A full pre-birth assessment will enable an informed decision to be made about future planning for the child and family.

Hart (2001) states that pre-birth assessments provide the opportunity to:

- identify and safeguard babies possibly most likely to suffer future significant harm;

- ensure that vulnerable parents are offered support at the start of their parenting rather than when difficulties have arisen;

- establish a working partnership with parents before the baby is born;

- assist parents with any problems that may impair their parenting capacity.

A range of issues will need to be considered as part of the assessment. This will include obtaining a full chronology of events and, if appropriate, gaining the parents' views and attitudes about any previous children who have been removed and evaluating what might have changed. It will be important for there to be a proactive approach to involve the father (including establishing paternity if required once the baby is born) and extended family members, as appropriate. If the outcome of the assessment is a decision to initiate care proceedings at birth, then active consideration should be given to the possibility of a concurrent care plan.

If a local authority has developed a specialist concurrent planning team, it may be appropriate for that team to take a role in working with the social worker for the family to undertake the pre-birth assessment. In any event, at an appropriate stage within the assessment, possibly at the pre-birth child protection conference or at a legal planning meeting, consideration should be given to making a referral to either an in-house or an external provider of concurrent placements.

The role of family group conferences

Local authorities should have protocols about the use of family group conferences as a part of their compliance with the pre-proceedings phase of the Public Law Outline. Any pre-birth assessment will need to take account of the wider family and friendship network, and as part of that work the social worker should complete a family tree or genogram. The use of family group conferences can be a positive and extremely helpful way of considering the potential involvement of the wider family and the role they could play with the parents and the child. If timing does not make this possible within the pre-birth period, then this should take place as soon as practicable after the baby's birth or when the plan for care proceedings in relation to an infant is being considered.

Family group conferences aim to support and empower families to find their own solutions to problems. The wider family network becomes a primary planning group in which they are encouraged to use their own strengths and resources to consider plans for the child. It is also an opportunity for them to be advised about available resources that could assist them with supporting an appropriate plan for the child. The focus will be on improving the family's understanding of the concerns and enabling them to be involved in the decision-making process, where possible. It may not be possible in some situations, within the pre-birth period, to organise a meeting with full attendance of all appropriate wider family and friends. However, it can be useful for the family group conference co-ordinator to discuss the aims and potential value of holding such a meeting directly with the parents and setting up a meeting with whoever in the wider network is available to take part.

An independent co-ordinator will undertake the preliminary work to set up the meeting, advising the parents and participants of the purpose of the meeting and how it will be organised. The co-ordinator can play an important role in helping the parents understand the potential value of the family group conference and encouraging them to identify people within their network who may be able to contribute to the care planning for their child. However, in some situations, it may be necessary to make specific arrangements for or to exclude a family member if, for example, there are concerns about a risk they may pose.

Usually only professionals who are directly involved will attend. Information sharing occurs at the start of the meeting, which is chaired by the co-ordinator. If there is a possibility of considering a plan for concurrency, it is vital that the attending social worker ensures all the participants understand what the reasons are for considering such a placement, what it would mean in practice and why the local authority plan includes adoption. Good social work practice requires that this information is provided in a straightforward, clear and culturally competent manner.

It is common practice for the family members attending to have some time on their own without the professionals present to consider the plan and a potential contingency plan, as appropriate. The social worker who presented the information would be advised of the family's plan and unless such a plan presents a significant risk to the child, it should be actively considered. Timescales and potential resources to support the plan should be discussed.

Viability of family and friends carers

In a situation where a decision to initiate care proceedings has been made, a family group conference may identify people within the wider network who could be assessed as either short-term or permanent carers for the child. The Children Act 1989 Guidance and Regulations *Volume 2: Care Planning, Placement and Case Review* (2010) and s22c of the Children Act 1989 require the local authority to consider the most appropriate placement when a placement with the child's parents is not possible. Chapter 3 of this guidance states:

> *In determining which is the most appropriate placement the local authority must "give preference to" a placement with a connected person, i.e. a relative, friend or other person connected with the child, reflecting the principle that children should, wherever possible, be brought up within their families and communities, if they cannot remain with their parents.*

It is therefore vital that at least initial viability work is undertaken to consider the potential for wider family group members to provide care to the child before a decision is made about pursuing a concurrent care plan. If there is a family member who may be able to provide an appropriate safe and nurturing home for the child, even if only in the short term at that stage, then concurrent planning would not be appropriate. It is often not possible to undertake a full assessment of a family member as a potential permanent carer within the timeframe available and it is also difficult for such family members to be expected to consider all the implications of such a care plan when they may be responding to a need for an immediate placement for a child.

DECISION MAKING ABOUT A CONCURRENT CARE PLAN

Where a decision has been made to initiate care proceedings and there are no appropriate carers within the wider family, an alternative placement with a concurrent carer should be actively considered as part of the care planning process. Assessment work undertaken pre-birth may indicate that a parent and child fostering placement or a residential resource may be appropriate. In such circumstances, consideration can be given to concurrency as a contingency plan. It may not be appropriate, however, for concurrent carers to remain linked with a child over a number of months while these other placement options are pursued. However, if a parent is assessed as not being in a position to make use of either of these placement resources, assessment work could continue with them in the community with the infant being placed with concurrent carers.

If the grounds for initiating care proceedings and separation from the birth parents are met and there are no suitable birth family members or friends as alternative carers, then a placement with concurrent carers can provide the most secure and nurturing family home for the baby whilst assessment work with the parents is undertaken. However, such a plan cannot proceed unless a suitable placement with concurrent carers has been identified. The social worker for the child must ensure that there is full and timely communication with the appropriate family-finding lead or manager who authorises concurrent placements – both those that are internal to the local authority or inter-agency placements.

Consideration could also be given to the option of a fostering for adoption care plan if the assessment work to date by the local authority has concluded that adoption is a very clear potential outcome of the care proceedings. If there are no appropriate concurrent carers available, the local authority should consider whether there are any approved prospective adopters who could meet the needs of the child and who may be able to provide a fostering placement until care proceedings are concluded. An additional report in relation to the capacity of the prospective adopters to provide an appropriate foster placement for the child will need to be prepared (see the section on fostering for adoption carers in Chapter 6).

Local authority protocols

Local authorities should develop clear written procedures and protocols in relation to the identification of potential concurrent planning referrals. Such procedures will link with the operational instructions for pre-birth assessments, viability assessments for potential family and friends carers and family group conferences. It can be helpful to develop a flowchart which identifies the processes from early referral, initial and core assessment through to legal planning meetings, Public Law Outline pre-proceedings meetings and pre-birth child protection conferences. (See Appendix 6 for an outline flowchart for concurrent planning referrals.)

Questions in relation to the potential for a concurrent care plan can be built into, for example, templates for recording legal planning meetings. Such protocols can be agreed within a steering group which should include key senior managers with appropriate input from the local authority legal team. Other considerations to include in such a protocol are how to ensure early notification to the relevant adoption manager of the potential need for a concurrent placement and the process for tracking and oversight of the decision making about such referrals.

There may also be merit in agreeing a local legal protocol in relation to transfer of such cases after care proceedings have been issued to the county court, and early notification to the local CAFCASS manager in order to ensure there is minimum delay in the progress of the case through the appropriate court.

Relinquished babies

There have been some instances where concurrent carers have been used as fostering placements for relinquished babies. Whilst this does not entirely fit with the concurrency model, as these placements are not being made within the framework of care proceedings, it may enable these babies to have a direct placement with carers approved to provide an adoptive home, if that continues to be the care plan. Concurrent carers will have been assessed as being capable of managing a significant degree of uncertainty and so should be best placed to care for a relinquished baby. In such situations, there may be very little known about the parents or wider family when the mother is requesting adoption. It may not be known at that stage whether there would be any grounds to intervene if the mother changes her mind and wishes the baby to be returned to her care. There may also be wider family group members able to step in who were not known about at the time of placement. There may have been little or no previous involvement with the mother prior to her giving birth and stating her wish to give up her baby. It is clearly essential that the mother is provided with full information about support services available and an opportunity for skilled counselling support to consider her decision carefully. Every situation will need to be considered carefully when determining the most appropriate placement for the baby in the immediate period following the mother's decision to relinquish care.

The potential for using a concurrent carer as a foster carer in such circumstances is worth active consideration from the baby's perspective. As a future possible adoptive placement, matching issues will need to be considered very carefully before a placement is made. The parent/s will need to be informed about the options for the baby to be placed with a foster carer who is also approved as an adoptive parent. This dual role should be taken into account when making contact arrangements. The carers will need to fully understand the difference between this as a fostering placement and one made within the framework of care proceedings for which they would have been prepared. In such situations, there may potentially be a higher likelihood of the baby returning to the care of parent/s or wider birth family.

MATCHING ISSUES

A placement with a concurrent carer has to take account of the fact that it is potentially the child's adoptive home. Careful consideration therefore needs to be given to matching issues. The process of matching is a skilled task and will take place within a much shorter timeframe than that normally allowed for prospective adoptive placements. There is unlikely to be full information about the child's needs, but there is the same requirement for the social worker to identify as much information as possible to enable an informed decision to be made by the local authority and the prospective concurrent carers. The local authority has a responsibility towards the child and the carers as the potential adoptive parents to ensure there is full disclosure of relevant background information concerning the child. The prospective concurrent carers need to be clearly advised that the information in relation to the child they are considering is confidential and complete an agreement to confirm their compliance with this.

The concurrent placement is made under fostering regulations and it is therefore not appropriate for these fostering placements to be considered by the adoption panel at this stage. However, the local authority will need to have established its own protocols and management decision making for agreeing such a placement. This protocol will need to include how the decision making about the concurrent placement is recorded to evidence how the child's needs and prospective carers' capacity to meet those needs has been taken fully into account. This process should also identify the particular support needs of the carers to enable them to meet the needs of the infant during the fostering phase. The same considerations need to be applied to fostering for adoption placements and local authority protocols should reflect this.

Quinton (2012), in his review of matching in adoption, commented on the fact that there is a lack of clarity about what exactly is meant in relation to the "needs" of children who need to be placed for adoption and a lack of clear evidence of how social workers assess those needs. He identifies that research on placement disruption makes it clear that adopters need to have six potential or established qualities:

...a commitment to children who are not birth children; a flexible and relaxed approach to parenting; realistic expectations; an ability to distance themselves from the child's behaviour, including tolerance of a lack of closeness; sensitivity to other attachments the child may have; and a willingness to work with the agency.

All these factors would be pertinent to prospective concurrency matches, alongside a proven and demonstrable capacity for resilience and emotional resourcefulness. Quinton also highlights the significance of support services and how these should be factored into the matching process. He says, 'Indeed, it is necessary to re-conceptualise the idea of matching capacity to needs to take support routinely into account' (2012).

There are particular matching issues that do need to be actively considered when deciding on a concurrency placement.

Geography

The location of the placement is very important and it is critical to consider not just the proximity to the parents but also to any other known significant family members. Any potential risk issues relating to the parents need to be factored in as part of the decision making. Reasonable proximity to the birth family may be manageable with a traditional fostering placement, but may be too risky for a potential adoptive placement. Some parents could be in temporary accommodation or living transient lives and this will need to be acknowledged with the prospective concurrent carers and considered when determining the appropriateness of the match. If the carers live within a reasonable distance of the birth family, other factors to take into account include whether they are registered with the same GP; whether they use the same shopping area; or whether an older child in the wider birth family attends the same school as the concurrent carers' child.

Distance from the contact venue is another factor. Most approved concurrent carers should live within a reasonable radius to avoid babies spending lengthy periods in cars or on public transport when travelling to contact. The details of how the infant will be transported to contact should be considered prior to a placement being made.

Ethnicity, culture and religion

At the point of considering a potential match, there may be limited knowledge about the child's ethnic, cultural or religious background. There may, for example, be no or limited information about the father's ethnicity or religion if the mother or others have not been able to provide information on his identity or if the father has not engaged with the assessment process. However, as much information as possible should be obtained to inform the matching process. The Statutory Guidance on Adoption in England and Wales, updated in February 2011, sets out matching considerations.

> *A prospective adopter can be matched with a child with whom they do not share the same ethnicity, provided they can meet the child's other identified needs. The core issue is what qualities, experiences and attributes the prospective adopter can draw on and their level of understanding of the discrimination and racism the child may be confronted with when growing up. This applies equally whether a child is placed with a black or minority ethnic family, a white family, or a family which includes members of different ethnic origins.*

Thus careful consideration needs to be given to the information that is known about the child's ethnic and cultural background and to how the prospective carers may be able to support the child to understand and maintain her or his heritage. Discussion will need to take place about the extent of information available, what this may mean for the child in the future and how the carers may support the child, not just as an infant but throughout her or his childhood, if adoption becomes the plan.

Health and development

For a baby placed directly from hospital after birth, there may be limited information about the relevant health and background history of the parents. In some situations the mother may have had minimal contact with antenatal services or the father may be unknown. In other situations, a parent may have had previous children removed and placed in foster care or adoption, and there may be considerable information that could be gathered quickly from local authority records. Information on the health and development of other full siblings would be of relevance.

The concurrent carers' capacity to manage this uncertainty should have been covered fully within their assessment so that it is known what the carers feel they definitely cannot manage or be helped to manage and what they would want to "have further discussion about". There may be information, for example, about the mother's drug use in pregnancy but not her alcohol use, as there may be a lack of confidence about her capacity to accurately report on the extent of alcohol use. Information about such matching considerations will have been discussed in detail with the prospective carers through the preparation and assessment stage and will need to be drawn upon to inform the decision making about the potential match.

Although there are often tight timescales for decision making, carers do need enough time to reflect on available information, read reports and to seek any further clarification, as appropriate. It is recommended good practice to enable the prospective carers to have the opportunity for a discussion with an appropriate medical practitioner. This may be the local authority medical adviser or perhaps the consultant nurse for looked after children or another appropriate paediatrician or neonatologist. (See the section below for a good practice example of the role of the medical adviser.)

Siblings

If there are older siblings who have already been placed for adoption, it is essential that their adopters are informed in a timely way about the birth and plans for the child. Local authorities should develop a protocol about how and when this information is shared, given the fact that this is confidential information about the birth family. It is often important for this information to be shared with the adopters of an older child before the new baby is born. This enables early discussion about whether they would wish to be considered if adoption becomes the plan for that child.

The adopters of the older child may feel able to consider the concurrency route for a second or third time around but will need help to explore the full implications of such a decision for the whole family. Some may feel that concurrency is not right for their family but would still wish to be assessed as prospective adoptive parents for the child if a plan for adoption is agreed. If there is the potential for the placement of a child with their older adopted sibling, and initial viability indicates that this is a real option for the child, then this should take priority over the opportunity to place the baby with a concurrent carer.

If concurrency is a possibility, the adopters will need to think through what it might mean for their child to have a younger sibling living with them on a fostering basis. That child may have no contact with their birth parents so, dependent on the age of the child, they will need to consider how contact arrangements will be managed by the family and explained to their adopted child. They will have to think through the implications for the placement of a sibling who returns to the birth parent and so has a very different life path to the one experienced by the adopted child.

The carer's particular circumstances

The prospective concurrent carers will need to consider at the time of placement any new or additional family or work commitments that may be of relevance to the concurrency process.

If the prospective carers have older children, they will have to think about the impact on them and how they will meet the differing needs of their children and the child being considered for placement. The timing of a placement might not fit if, for example, an older child in the family is just getting ready for a move into primary school, or it may fit very well if a child is settled into nursery or school, and the carer feels confident in being able to manage the demands of the contact arrangements.

The potential duration of the care proceedings and contact commitments must be considered in terms of any significant predictable family event, work or other commitments. Plans to move house or undertake a big loft extension may need to be put on hold. Whilst it may sometimes be unavoidable for babies in traditional foster placements to have periods with a respite carer, this would not be the expectation or appropriate for a child placed with a concurrent carer.

RISK ASSESSMENT

It is good practice for a risk assessment to be completed as part of a referral for a child who needs a fostering placement. This risk assessment facilitates information gathering and analysis of the parents' or birth family's circumstances and informs decision making about an appropriate match. This process should also be undertaken in relation to a potential concurrency match.

If there are significant concerns about the risk a birth family member may present, a decision could be made that the concurrent carers will not be involved in transporting the child to contact and meeting the parents at handover. In this situation, the child should be transported by a consistent member of staff – ideally the person involved in contact supervision (see Chapter 7 for more information).

The risk assessment needs to be kept under review as the placement progresses. Identified risks to the placement may lessen if the parents positively engage with the assessment or if there are other changes in their circumstances. It may then be possible for the carers to have a role in contact with the parents in a safe way for all concerned. If not, a handover or contact book can be set up so that the carers can provide written information about the baby's development, routines and preferences for the parents to make use of at contact.

Risk assessments may also need to take into account new issues that indicate that additional measures need to be put in place to ensure the safety and confidentiality of the carers as prospective adopters (see the section on confidentiality in Chapter 8).

Prospective concurrent carers may be single or part of a couple, lesbian, gay or heterosexual, with or without children and the information contained within the risk assessment needs to be considered alongside the profile of the potential carers when determining whether the match should go ahead. It should also consider whether any additional measures need to be put into place to protect the carers, their family and the child.

Providing medical advice in concurrent planning – experience in Brighton and Hove

This information has been provided by Dr Sian Bennett, Clinical Director, Brighton and Hove Children and Family Services.

Concurrent planning adds another dimension when providing medical advice to social workers and carers. Adoption by the traditional route allows for the collection of available medical information, assessment of the child and requesting of additional information or investigation, if needed. However, the nature of concurrency means that placement of the child will take place before this process can be concluded. Often vulnerable babies may be placed directly from hospital (some have been only hours old). Providing medical advice in concurrent planning therefore requires strong multi-agency working with social work and medical professionals. They need to understand all the issues from each other's perspectives in order to best support the children, parents and concurrent carers.

The provision of medical advice in Brighton and Hove has evolved to take account of these challenges and to make best use of the skills of the Looked After Children (LAC) Health Team, which is multidisciplinary, with specialist nurses and community paediatricians working together closely. Additionally, since 2007, community child health services have been integrated with children's social care services, which has enabled a more streamlined approach with better communication and information sharing between professionals.

The key areas of input by the medical adviser to the concurrency process have developed to include the following.

1 Participation in adoption preparation groups

The medical adviser participates in the adoption preparation groups, presenting the medical factors which are important for children who are placed for adoption, either by the traditional route or concurrently. Background factors such as maternal drug and alcohol misuse, risks of blood-borne virus infections, parental learning difficulties and mental health problems are relevant for all children being placed for adoption. These factors are explored using case histories to promote discussion and give prospective carers the opportunity to ask questions. Written information is provided, with a reading list of helpful background information. The issues of consent in gathering medical information from and about birth families and the constraints this brings are emphasised. This helps prospective applicants to develop a realistic understanding of these, and of the extra challenges in providing timely health information in concurrent planning.

2 Flexibility in meeting with concurrent carers

The medical adviser is available to meet with the concurrent carers and to share what health information is available or to facilitate a meeting with the neonatal team, if the baby has been receiving treatment, such as monitoring of drug withdrawal, on the

Special Care Baby Unit. Themes that were discussed during the preparation groups can be elaborated upon and made relevant to the individual baby's situation. A key aspect is to help carers understand the uncertainties of the future prognosis, especially if there have been significant issues involving antenatal drug and alcohol exposure, and to present a balanced picture of the risks which are known, based on evidence from research and personal practice.

3 Integrated model of the LAC Health Team

At the same time as concurrent planning was first implemented in Brighton and Hove, a Consultant Nurse role for looked after children was developed, with a focus on raising the standard of knowledge and health advice for all children in care. Other nurses have been added to the team to undertake statutory health assessments and prepare health care plans. The team works closely with family health visitors and directly supports carers and birth parents of children with more complex presentations.

4 Accelerated access to the Child Development Team

Many of the children placed concurrently are vulnerable babies who have experienced adverse antenatal factors. Local protocols have been developed so that babies who have received specialist neonatal care for drug withdrawal or who are at risk of foetal alcohol spectrum disorders are seen by the medical adviser, both for the purpose of preparing medical advice and for fast-tracking to the multidisciplinary child development team, if appropriate. This avoids delay and early advice from therapists is facilitated. Sometimes serious health or developmental conditions have emerged over time, which could not have been predicted from the health information originally available. The early attachments and commitment to the child that concurrent carers have developed improve their understanding of the child's needs.

5 Post-adoption support

Often questions about health and developmental issues arise for concurrent carers after they have adopted and they welcome the opportunity to have further discussion with the medical adviser. As children adopted from Brighton and Hove often remain relatively local, this allows for continuity with the local health teams and access to the medical adviser can be arranged. Families have found it helpful to review the early health history again and to consider it more specifically in relation to the progress their child is making. Sometimes it is necessary to undertake further clinical and developmental assessments which may reveal new information.

In summary, medical advice for children placed concurrently poses different challenges, and, as a group, the children often have complex backgrounds and adverse antenatal experiences. Our practice has developed to ensure proactive and timely health support to these vulnerable babies and to offer flexible and responsive advice both to concurrent carers, parents and professionals working with them.

THE ROLE OF THE SUPERVISING SOCIAL WORKER IN THE MATCHING PROCESS

The supervising social worker for the concurrent carers must ensure that they are provided with all appropriate information about the child in order to provide active support to them in managing any issues that might arise. The worker should accompany the carers to key meetings and be available for debriefing discussions afterwards.

Whilst decisions need to be made within a very short timescale, the worker needs to act in a supportive and protective capacity to allow the prospective carers time to discuss the information and seek answers to any questions they may have. There may be no clear information about whether a concurrent care plan will definitely go ahead. The baby may not yet be born if it has been possible to do the planning for the match pre-birth. The carers have to manage a great deal of information about a child they may go on to adopt within a context of significant uncertainty about whether the plan will proceed.

Concurrent carers will inevitably start bonding with the child being considered as well as anticipating the eventual outcome of the placement. They may need to start talking to older children in their family about the plan or key relatives within their support network. They may have to alert employers to the fact that they will need to cease their employment at short notice or commence a period of unpaid or special leave. These are all circumstances that the supervising social worker should have helped the carers think through and prepare for but the reality will inevitably bring new challenges and possibly an intensity of feelings that had not been anticipated.

The supervising social worker will need to provide responsive and proactive support and be available to provide input to older children in the family or other people in the carers' network, as appropriate. The carers will need advice on how to manage the confidential information they have received about the birth family whilst accessing appropriate support from key friends and family. The social worker must ensure that the carers receive regular updating information about the baby and the progress in the care planning.

There may be a number of outcomes that the supervising social worker will have to prepare the concurrent carers for and support them with.

- If the match is being considered pre-birth, there may be unforeseen complications or very specific health issues that cause the concurrent care plan decision to be revised. The carers need to know that they can also change their minds in the light of such new information.

- There may be changes to the parents' circumstances immediately following the birth of a child which could cause the local authority to reconsider the care plan. For example, a mother who had been refusing to consider the risks her partner posed to her and the baby may make a different decision after the baby is born and ask for the opportunity to live with her baby in a parent and child foster placement.

- New information may come forward about a potential family and friends carer that would need active consideration before a concurrent care plan could proceed.

- The care plan for concurrency may not be agreed in court and it may or may not be appropriate to retain the link with the concurrent carers as a contingency plan, for example, when there is a plan for a parent and child fostering placement.

The prospective carers will have to manage absorbing a great deal of information and undertake considerable planning and preparation over a short time period. They may have to cope with a change of plan and a different decision being made about the child they expected to be caring for, involving a range of feelings from excitement, anticipation and possibly frustration, anxiety and loss. Skilled support will be needed for the carers and their wider network through this phase. For some, the decision-making process may be spread over a few weeks and there will be a need for some recovery time before they may be ready to be approached again about another potential placement. The carers may need support in reversing work plans if they had already prepared their employers for their departure.

The carers will need to acquire essential baby equipment and may have to be advised just to borrow the basics at the outset until it is clear that the baby will definitely be placed.

TRANSITION PLANNING

Dependent on the age of the infant, there should be a meeting to plan the transition if the care plan for concurrency is agreed in court. If the placement is to be made directly from the hospital, a detailed birth plan should be drawn up by the social worker for the child to be included in the hospital notes for the baby. The hospital midwifery service will need to be kept fully informed and updated. The carers may be involved in meeting the baby at the hospital and perhaps be involved in gaining advice and support from staff on a special care baby unit. The opportunity for the carers to meet the baby and have an initial meeting with the parents needs to be carefully planned once the court has endorsed the plan. Any introduction time the carers may have with the baby at the hospital will need to be co-ordinated around the contact times for the parents.

If the baby has already been moved to a short-term foster placement or is a slightly older infant in foster care, an introductions planning meeting should be held to plan the transition from the foster carer. Good practice in relation to managing and co-ordinating the transition should still be adhered to, albeit often in a more contracted timeframe. Full information on the routines and care of the infant should be provided by the current foster carer with the opportunity for the concurrent carers to assume some of the day-to-day caring tasks for the baby within the foster carers' home. The supervising social worker should work closely with the social worker for the child and together they will need to oversee the transition planning. Prospective concurrent carers still need the opportunity to express any doubts or ask any further questions they might have about the plans.

The concurrent carers should be provided with full written information about the child and it is the supervising social worker's responsibility to ensure they have all the information and guidance needed to undertake the fostering task.

The National Fostering Minimum Standards 2011 state:

> Prior to the placement of each child, the foster carer is provided with all the information held by the fostering service that they need to carry out their role effectively. The information is provided in a clear, comprehensive written form and includes the support that will be available to the carer.

A foster carer agreement and specific placement agreement will need to be completed and the supervising social worker should ensure the carers understand the process for forthcoming meetings in respect of the child, i.e. LAC review meetings, medical assessments, etc.

The local authority adoption service or the voluntary adoption agency must ensure that operational instructions include arrangements for making concurrent placements. Supervising social workers should have checklists to ensure that all the appropriate information has been provided to the carers and that the carers are clear about the respective roles of the supervising social worker and the social worker for the child, particularly if they are not working as part of a specialist concurrency team.

The role of the supervising social worker once the placement is underway is covered in more detail in Chapter 6 and in relation to contact in Chapter 7.

WORK WITH PARENTS

It is essential that the child's parents are provided with a proactive and responsive service. The stakes could not be higher for the parents and they need to have clear information about the plan for their child, the expectations of them and the support services that will be available. Some parents will be able to make the changes in their lives to enable their child to be safely rehabilitated to their care. Others may be able to use the experience to start the process of making changes to ensure that they can care for future children.

If there has been an opportunity for a full pre-birth assessment, the parents should have been given clear information about the assessment process, the expectations of them and support services they can or are expected to access. There needs to be an evidence-based approach to the work that focuses on clear analysis of the risks, interventions provided and outcomes that are required.

If concurrency becomes a potential plan, the child's parents need to be provided with full information about what this means and given written information which explains the status of the carers who will be fostering their child. This material should also be provided to their lawyers. One of the key principles of concurrent planning is the need for transparency, and whilst it may be difficult for the parents initially to accept that their child is being cared for by foster carers able and willing to adopt their child if that becomes the plan, it is essential that the potential benefits for the child of this plan are fully explained. A plan for concurrency would not be considered by the local authority unless there was clear evidence of sufficient concern about the parents' circumstances to warrant not just issuing care proceedings but also a plan for separation, with adoption as a potential outcome if changes cannot be made within the child's timeframe. The detail of the plan for further assessment work and parenting skills work will be agreed within the court framework.

Ward *et al* (2012) noted that a number of parents described experiencing a "wake-up call" when they realised that they would have to make changes in order to parent successfully. A plan for concurrency which underlines for the parents the potential for their child to be adopted if changes are not made, plus the provision of appropriate focused parenting support services, may provide that incentive or "wake-up call".

The President of the Family Division said in 2006:

> Concurrent planning has built into it the need for recognition by the parents that failure by them to address their underlying problems means that the local authority will then recommend to the court that their child is placed permanently with concurrent carers for adoption. Clear messages to this effect must be given by professionals. There must be a glimmer of hope of rehabilitation. Parents must be made aware of the

results of the initial assessment of their difficulties and what they would be expected to achieve before the child could return. The outcome would rest on their response rather than on previous history.

(The Rt Hon Sir Mark Potter, 2006)

The child's parents need to know that all the workers involved in the concurrent planning placement will be open and honest with them and will communicate with each other. The nature and process of all aspects of the assessment should be fully explained. They will need to be told at regular intervals what progress they are making and what work is still outstanding, and timescales should be clearly spelt out. The need to avoid drift and inaction and the consequences of this, for example, missing contact or not keeping appointments with other services, should be pointed out and followed up immediately by the workers involved.

Parents must be provided with skilled, sensitive support throughout the concurrency process. They will need to be encouraged and supported to access the support services available and all the workers involved should be very sensitive to the particular status of the placement and the feelings this may evoke for the parents. All parents where the local authority is considering a plan for adoption should have access to a skilled professional who is not part of the decision-making process. The parents should be actively encouraged to access such support and this should be detailed in any information provided to parents about concurrent planning.

If the assessment and parenting skills work progress positively and rehabilitation is a clear potential plan, the child's parents must continue to be provided with full information about the stages towards rehabilitation, the process of decision making, the expectations of them and the supervision and support that will continue to be available as part of that plan.

If the plan becomes one of adoption, again, the social worker for the child has a clear responsibility to ensure that parents are provided with and encouraged and facilitated to access appropriate counselling and support services. Consideration should be given to a support strategy that may enable the parents to continue to make changes to enable a different outcome for any future children.

There has been little reported information on the experience of birth parents of the concurrency process. The early evaluation work of the three teams in England by Monck *et al* (2003) did involve some interviews with birth parents (13 sets of birth parents with children placed with concurrent carers). The parents interviewed had a range of experiences and some felt concerned at that time that they had been given little written information about the scheme before their children were placed. Some parents expressed upset and anger about their experience of concurrency, feeling that they had not been given a proper chance to demonstrate their capacity to care for their children.

When they first said concurrent planning, I was against it. I dunno why, I just don't like it. They were saying, 'Right, he is going to concurrency carers'. That's like saying, 'Well, we're not going to give you a chance.'

Another parent had a different experience, and said:

I liked the carers when I first met them...They kept a diary for me of the baby's sleeping and feeding, and so on. They showed me the diary whenever we had contact. Later: *I wrote to the judge saying that the baby could be adopted only if he could go to the concurrency carers, as I know they love him.*

This is an extract from an account by one mother of her experience of concurrent planning and her involvement in the decision making about the plans for her infant.

And then it all began. Contact four times a week, solicitors' meetings, court hearings, LAC reviews, assessments, interviews with psychologists, housing issues and more. It was relentless. How could I get through all this? I did not like my social worker – she was too young, inexperienced, judgemental, I thought. My opinion changed. She worked with me and supported me. She worked closely with other agencies. She sorted out my housing and helped me acquire a new home. I also had another worker who supervised my contact. Together we worked really hard on my rehabilitation, things were moving in the right direction – all the team hoped mother and baby would be reunited.

I successfully completed rehab and the timescales imposed were closing in. My social worker applied to the court for more time in the care proceedings. I was now seriously considering the future for me and all of my children. After looking realistically at the bigger picture, I had to look at my teenage children, they had suffered emotional neglect.

This was the first time I had to make some real decisions in my life. I was now ready to take responsibility for my life instead of being in the hands of professionals. I had to look at my teenage daughters who had suffered emotional abuse and for the first time I would be able to look after them – my middle child wondered why I had cleaned up my act only for the baby – why didn't I do it for her? For myself I was quietly afraid of relapse and the consequences of relapse on all of us, including the baby. I knew that the carer loved my baby who was clearly attached to her.

This helped me to a decision based on the needs of my children, something I had not done before. Would I be thought of as selfish and hard? The workers seemed to know my thoughts and said I was not a bad person for thinking this. They helped me tell the older children – their reaction was a mixture of anger and silent relief but we were able to talk about it as a family – a new experience. What helped us was knowing we would have direct contact twice a year after adoption. I knew I had done the right thing for all of my children.

From concurrency I have a new life with choices and freedom and continue a relationship with the team. My child was a gift to me and she was my gift to her adopted mother.

Coram Policy and Research Unit (Laws *et al*, 2012) have undertaken some research on the outcomes for children placed concurrently and this included contacting the families of children who had been rehabilitated following a placement with concurrent carers. In one of these situations, the child was returned to an extended family member.

Rachel was referred soon after birth, and placed in a concurrent planning placement at eight weeks old. The birth mother initially attended some contact sessions, but did not sustain this. The aunt's account, from her point of view, is as follows: she and the wider family were initially unable to care for Rachel – they were already looking after the birth mother's older child, the grandmother was working and the aunt was studying. Rachel is now stably placed within her extended family, the aunt who cares for her reports that she is doing well although she does need some additional help at school.

She stated: 'We fell out with social services, and were not happy to work with them, so that's when they brought Coram in, to work between the family and social services. Coram explained all the processes we should follow and supervised things between the family and social services... At first I was reluctant to see Rachel because I was disappointed with my sister – this was the second mistake she had made. Coram kept speaking to me about it and eventually on one of the visits I saw Rachel and as soon as I saw her my anger went away and I cried in the hall and from then on I was in love with Rachel...If Rachel had been adopted we wouldn't know how she was doing. Would have been a regret. Pleased that she is part of family life. If she had been adopted we would have wondered if it was the right decision. Very happy with the decision we made – think it was the best decision.

DECISION MAKING ABOUT THE FINAL CARE PLAN

The concurrent carers will have been kept closely informed about the progress of the assessment of the parents. During the course of the placement they may have met with the Children's Guardian and, in some situations, an expert undertaking an assessment within the proceedings. The carers may have established a relationship with the parents through contact and have a good understanding of the potential likely outcome. For example, they may be aware that the mother has resumed a relationship with a risky violent partner or a parent has relapsed into drug use and perhaps has not been attending contact regularly.

If the assessment has been progressing positively, the carers will understand that contact may be increasing or moving to the parent's home as part of the rehabilitation plan. In such circumstances, the carers will need considerable support to stay focused on the child and may need to be provided with additional external counselling support.

Carers will need to be reminded of the stages of the decision-making process for the child within the local authority and by the court. If the plan is to be adoption, the usual procedures in relation to consideration of an adoptive match should be followed with the carers. The placement will remain a fostering placement until the conclusion of the care proceedings and the making of the placement order. This adoption placement will need to be presented to the local authority adoption panel and this can take place immediately following the final hearing.

The transition for the concurrent carers from being foster carers for a child to becoming prospective adoptive and then adoptive parents can be a complex and emotionally demanding one. Carers may have adapted to "being in foster care mode" and keeping their emotions in check. They may have developed a good working relationship with the birth parents and feel a mixture of extreme relief about the outcome given their hopes of becoming an adoptive family, but also empathy and upset for the birth family and the child.

The normal adoption planning process in relation to decision making about the concurrent carers as prospective adopters may be helpful to the carers in making that transition. The supervising social worker may have to provide particular input focusing on this change of role and support for the carers in managing the intensity of feelings involved. The process of farewell contacts is detailed in Chapter 7.

After hours of contact, hours of juggling our lives, we barely had time to register, let alone contemplate, the impossible gap between loving her unequivocally, embracing her wholeheartedly into the family, while accepting that she might go back to her birth family and we would never see her again.

The assessment of her parents and endless court hearings were finally completed and the judge decided just nine months after she had been placed with us that the best place for Stella was to stay with us...At the adoption hearing our birth daughter Amy, then six years, loved the attention the judge gave both girls and Stella left the court the proud owner of a beautiful new balloon.

As a result of concurrency and regular meetings over a period of months with Stella's parents, we will hopefully one day be able to do what so few adoptive parents can do and talk about her birth parents as real people. In this way we hope to help her understand the difference between the reality and fantasy of who they are and why they did what they did.

(Brighton and Hove concurrency adopter)

6

Recruiting, assessing, supervising and supporting concurrent carers

When the pioneering concurrent planning teams were being set up in England, there was considerable scepticism about whether carers could be recruited for this challenging and demanding task. The teams had to focus on recruiting prospective adopters who were prepared to manage significant uncertainty. There was uncertainty not just about the outcome of the court process and the final plan for the child in their care but also about the health and development of the child. Babies would be placed with carers on a fostering basis, possibly directly from hospital, with potentially very little background information and without the benefit of information from a pre-adoption medical. However, despite the demands of the recruitment challenge, all the teams experienced considerable success in recruiting carers able to take on this particular role. This chapter explores practice in relation to the recruitment, training and assessment of prospective carers, and support and supervision for approved carers.

RECRUITMENT

Concurrent planning will need an identified and specific profile within the local authority or adoption agency recruitment strategy. The concept of concurrent planning is sometimes not clearly understood. It is unlikely that many prospective adopters will approach an agency with a specific interest in or a detailed understanding of concurrency as a potential route to adoption.

Leaflets on concurrent planning and dedicated sections on the recruitment pages of the adoption agency website describing the role, with input from experienced concurrency adopters, will be essential to help to bring the approach alive. This may be challenging for new agencies setting up a scheme, but information or quotes could be obtained from existing teams or publications.

Staff who respond to initial enquiries from prospective adopters will themselves need a good understanding of concurrent planning and a belief in the role it can play as a permanence planning option. Referrals to the recruitment team will need to be followed up in a timely manner to ensure that all those with an initial interest in becoming a concurrency carer are quickly engaged in the process and provided with more detailed information and exploration of the issues.

There is no single profile for prospective concurrent carers and recruitment information should reinforce this. Prospective concurrency carers may be single, gay or lesbian, childless couples or experienced parents. Concurrency may also be an appropriate potential route for some second-time or even third-time adopters who feel they have the capacity to consider this.

It may be appropriate to also consider approaching approved adopters to gauge their interest in undertaking some additional preparation and assessment to enable them to be approved as concurrent carers.

> *A group of concurrency adopters in Brighton and Hove reflecting on their experiences all said that they did not know anything or very little about the scheme when they made their first enquiry. Some were very unsure about whether there might even be the possibility of babies needing adoptive homes. One adopter described their decision to adopt a baby through intercountry adoption until they contacted Brighton and Hove and found out about the concurrent planning scheme.*

It is clear from the experience in the US and the UK that the possibility for prospective adopters of having a young baby placed rather than a toddler or older child is a strong motivating factor. In addition, there is also considerable evidence that prospective carers are attracted to the general child-centred philosophy underpinning the concurrent planning model.

> *If the child returned to birth parents that was a risk for us. OK, while we might be bereaved, disappointed, upset, we could hopefully feel we had taken part in a positive process and that if the child did go back to parents that was the best thing. I think we both knew that concurrency was the better route. Perhaps not for us but for the child, yes.*
>
> (Concurrency adopter in Monck *et al*, 2003)

> *Once the principles were explained it just made sense as it put the child at the centre. We felt it was right for us although concurrency is not right for every prospective adopter, as it is not right for every child that needs an adoptive family.*
>
> (Brighton and Hove concurrency adopter)

I'd read a lot about adoption prior to contacting Coram. I'd read about attachment before eight months. And the whole concept of concurrent planning appealed to me. Seems right for the child, right for the parent.

(Coram concurrency adopter)

We both really honed in on concurrent planning because it fitted with our views, from our professional lives, about what is best for children and it made complete sense to us that children would be placed in the place that might become permanent, and that it was the adults that bore the anxiety and changes and not the child.

(Coram concurrency adopter)

The potential for the prospective concurrency adopters to establish a limited relationship with the birth parents was also cited as a factor that attracted carers to the scheme once they had had more time to consider the process and its implications in detail. Concurrency adopters described feeling positive about the potential for them to be better equipped to support their adopted child to make sense of their background if they had the opportunity to develop an acquaintance with and greater knowledge of the birth parents through their meetings at contact handover times.

I was hoping to get to know the birth parents so I could fill in the gaps, at the very least for the child and there was hope for more ongoing contact with them – I know adults who've been adopted and they struggle, there's an identity gap, and they search for birth parents around their adolescence. I was hoping to "hold" the whole family story and identity for her.

(Coram concurrency adopter)

The location of potential prospective carers is an important issue to consider within the recruitment strategy. Concurrent carers will need to live within a reasonable radius of the contact centre so that babies are not travelling long distances for contact. There may be many benefits for the child of being placed locally but there will also need to be careful consideration of any risks associated with such a plan. However, the need for children to be placed within an approximate 20 mile radius or a maximum 30 minute travelling time to the contact centre should not be an obstacle to developing a concurrency service and there is considerable experience within adoption agencies of managing local adoptive placements safely for many children and their families. The issue of location of concurrency carers when considering a match is explored more fully in Chapter 5.

Concurrent planning is described by Coram to enquirers as a "win-win" placement for the babies concerned, who will have the opportunity to develop secure attachments with their carers whilst still maintaining close contact with their birth parents.

The great advantage for the children concerned is that if they cannot go back to their birth family, it will prevent them having to suffer the upset and loss of moving from a foster home where they have settled to an adoptive family. They will be able to put down their roots and bond with their family from an early stage.

For concurrent carers who go on to adopt, the advantage is that they will have got to know and love their child from a very young age, and will have helped them through the early, unsettling months when plans were still uncertain.

We are looking for loving, emotionally resourceful families who can put the needs of very young children first and who can respect and work with the children's families in the early months.

We expect that many of the families will go on to adopt the children they have cared for. They will be in the very special position of having established a relationship with the child's parents so that they can understand the difficulties their child's birth families have struggled with.

(Extract from Coram recruitment information leaflet for prospective concurrent carers)

Checklist for recruitment

- Include a specific focus on concurrent planning within adoption recruitment strategy.

- Ensure that staff responsible for recruitment are fully briefed and confident about explaining concurrency as a potential route to adoption.

- Provide clear, specific information on concurrency on the recruitment pages of the adoption agency website and include positive and inclusive statements about the wide profile of potential concurrency carers.

- Provide specific leaflets/downloadable information sheets for prospective concurrent carers highlighting what concurrency entails and the benefits for the child.

- Ensure concurrency is profiled at information sessions and other recruitment events.

- Use quotes from experienced concurrent adopters within recruitment material and, if possible, input from them at recruitment events.

Preparation training

Preparation training for prospective concurrent carers will need to include everything that would be part of training for mainstream adopters, plus an additional component to cover the concurrency process and fostering task. Any online training materials provided for prospective carers prior to attending the preparation group will need to include relevant information for prospective concurrent carers. All adoption agencies are now considering their development of online information and training material to enable prospective carers to gain as much information as possible during the first stage of the preparation and assessment phase.

The additional components in the training should include clarification of the concurrency model, the responsibilities of carers during the fostering phase, contact and the legal procedures involved. It should also focus on the particular challenges relating to the uncertainty both about the outcome for and the health and development of the child. Most of the topics in the additional training component will need to be discussed within the preparation training sessions but then returned to and considered in more depth during the assessment.

There may be applicants attending preparation training who are still very unclear about whether concurrency would be the right route for them. They will need the reassurance that if they opt to be assessed for concurrency, they can still change their minds and be assessed as mainstream adopters if they decide during the process that concurrency is not right for them. Similarly, the agency may also advise during the assessment that concurrency may not be the right route for the applicants. Applicants need to understand that, if approved, they will be approved as both foster carers and adopters. Therefore, if a concurrent placement is not made, prospective adopters would still be considered for a mainstream adoption placement.

As with all preparation training, it is helpful to plan interactive exercises and to consider case scenarios or role plays to bring the material to life and to engage the applicants. Input from experienced concurrent carers can be very helpful. Consideration could also be given to providing input from an experienced foster carer who would be able to describe what it feels like to manage the involvement of a range of professionals in their lives, the responsibilities but also the challenges and frustrations of the fostering task. Experienced foster carers will also be able to provide information about the relationship they may develop with birth parents or other birth family members and the range of feelings that this may engender. Although the role of the mainstream foster carer is different, they may be able to offer a valuable insight into some aspects of the fostering task.

It is also important to give a voice to the perspective of the birth family within the preparation training by whatever method is possible and appropriate. Careful thought should be given to this.

However, there are particular issues for concurrent carers which are different from those normally experienced by foster carers, as they are potentially the adoptive parents of the child. As potential parents, they are likely to experience a complex range of emotions about the role and the relationship they are developing with the child and the birth family, and this needs to be acknowledged within the preparation training and developed further within the assessment process.

Certain aspects of the concurrency task should be highlighted; in particular, the fact that during the fostering phase the carers may feel powerless in the process and feel that their lives are "on hold" whilst the assessment work with the birth family is progressing and the outcome of the care proceedings is uncertain.

Much of the health input may be covered within the regular content of preparation training for prospective adopters. However, it is important to ensure that there is particular input on the needs of very young babies who may be born suffering from drug withdrawal. Input from a foster carer who has experienced caring for a withdrawing baby may be valuable and informative, as well as additional health input from the medical adviser to the agency/neonatal or paediatric practitioner or experienced nurse for looked after children.

We felt overwhelmed at times listening to the paediatrician's tales of just how traumatising it is to cope with a tiny baby born addicted to hard drugs or to cope with the varying and ongoing demands of a child taken into care because they had been neglected or physically or sexually assaulted. For the first time, these meetings also gave us the chance to meet concurrent carers who had been through the process already and knew some of what to expect. We fell on them, hanging on their every word about how they had coped, particularly when faced with meeting birth parents. By the end of the week, as well as making new friends we were armed with enough information to ensure we could never be under any illusion that concurrency was going to be an easy ride and we let social services know that we were ready to start on the next step – the assessment process.

(Brighton and Hove concurrency adopter)

The training for concurrency was a big reality check, so we followed that, we were very sort of cautious in a way.

(Coram concurrency adopter)

Additional components of preparation training

The concurrent planning model
- Concurrency – what it is and the key principles.
- The children who may be considered for concurrency and the matching process.
- Assessment work with the birth parents and extended family and how the carers will be kept informed of progress.

The fostering role

- The expectations of foster carers and the fostering regulatory framework.
- The role of the local authority in relation to parental responsibility for the child.
- The limitations of the foster carer role and feelings this can engender.
- Foster care agreements/safe caring guidelines.
- Foster care allowances, how much it is and for how long it will be paid.
- The role of the supervising social worker and visiting schedule – professional scrutiny and accountability alongside the support role.
- Responsibilities in relation to record keeping and communication with the supervising social worker and other professionals involved.
- The role of the social worker for the child/Independent Reviewing Officer and looked after children review process.
- The role of health professionals/health visitor and the nurse for looked after children – the potential for attendance at medical appointments alongside the birth parents.
- Confidentiality and responsibility of the carers in relation to information about the child and birth family, as well as the agency's responsibility in relation to information about the carers.

Motivation

- Consideration of the carers' motivation to pursue the concurrency route.
- Benefits and particular challenges for all parties in the process.
- The potential outcomes of a concurrent placement and consideration of how the carers may manage a plan for rehabilitation.

Needs of vulnerable infants

- The reality of caring for a vulnerable baby.
- Babies born with neonatal abstinence syndrome.
- The effects on babies of exposure to drugs and alcohol in utero.
- Early brain development and the need babies have for sensitive and consistent care.
- The importance of attunement and the value for the baby of a secure attachment relationship with the carer, including acknowledgement that the baby's primary attachment relationship will be with their carers, even though they may be retaining regular contact with their birth parents.

Contact

- The role contact plays in a concurrent placement/likely frequency and how this is kept under review.
- The expectations of all parties in relation to contact.
- What it might feel like for the concurrent carer handing over the baby at contact times/practicality of handover arrangements and the support carers will have and may need.

- The baby's needs and how contact can be managed to minimise the disruption to the baby/the role of the contact supervisor and social worker for the child.
- The practical demands of contact and the priority it will have to take in the carers' lives.
- What contact may be like for the birth parents and how they may feel about building a bond with their baby under the supervision and scrutiny of social work staff. How the parents may feel about the relationship with carers, knowing they are able to adopt the baby if that is the outcome of the court process.

Legal framework
- Outline of the legal framework for concurrent placements.
- The role of the social worker for the child and CAFCASS Guardian. The contact that the Guardian may have with the carer in their home.
- The process of assessment of the birth family/potential for expert assessments.
- Outline of timeframe for the care proceedings.
- The fact that the carers have no voice in care proceedings.
- The process of decision making about the local authority final care plan.
- If rehabilitation to the birth family is the outcome of court proceedings, how this would be planned and implemented.
- If a care plan for adoption is the outcome of court proceedings, the next steps between adoption placement and adoption order, including the timing and process for the adoption application.

Support needs
- The stresses and demands of the role. Managing a sustained level of uncertainty throughout the court process and the support carers and other close members of their family may need.
- Support from the supervising social worker and what this is likely to include.
- Potential support from other carers/friends and family.
- The role of a support group, if the agency is able to provide that.
- Support around contact – if the applicants are a couple, how might this be managed? For single applicants, there may be a need for additional support from within their close family and friendship network.
- The realities of managing the fostering task whilst also being the prospective adopters for the child – potentially managing very difficult strong feelings, e.g. a deepening attachment and love for the baby and empathy for the birth parents.

When reflecting on their preparation training for the task, experienced concurrency adopters from Brighton and Hove felt that whilst there was a significant emphasis on the fostering role, nothing really prepared them for the task and the feeling that they were "just" foster carers and that they were undertaking a job. This feeling came out particularly in relation to managing the demands of contact. Like mainstream foster carers, they also felt constrained in how much they could express their frustrations about the fostering role with their supervising social worker, given the vulnerability of their position. One adopter said that she found one of the most difficult tasks was managing a LAC review as a foster carer with birth parents attending – she said that it might have been helpful to have had the chance to role-play a LAC review or have had a fuller briefing beforehand about what to expect and what it might feel like to be a foster carer in such a meeting.

The point about the child going back was raised on a lot of occasions. But I think it's necessary. It has to be in your mind all the time, it is part of concurrency planning. Yes, we knew that children wouldn't be placed unless the chances of them returning were quite low, so the prognosis for that wasn't good.

(Concurrency adopter in Monck *et al*, 2003)

ASSESSMENT

The home study assessment builds on the foundations laid during the preparation training. It is important for the assessing social worker to demonstrate within the assessment report that all aspects of the concurrency task have been fully covered and evidence the applicants' capacity to manage the challenges of the role. Issues relating to the concurrency task need to be interwoven into the assessment report, as appropriate. Agencies may wish to consider supplementing the prospective adopters' report template to give some additional prompts for assessing social workers.

From July 2013, the two-stage adopter approval process will come into effect in England. Stage 1 is the pre-assessment process and should take two months. Stage 2 comprises the more intensive preparation and training and should be completed within four months, and ends with the agency decision. Prospective adopters can take a break of up to six months between the two stages. This is a part of a range of measures aimed at increasing the numbers of potential adoptive parents. The assessment process and report will be streamlined, with a strong emphasis on a focused and clear analysis of the evidence of the suitability to adopt. Prospective concurrent carers will need to have a written agreement at the outset of the assessment about the components of the assessment and the potential timescale for the work. They need to know how aspects relating to the concurrency task will be considered within the outline plan for the assessment, and be given the opportunity to increase their knowledge by provision of appropriate reading material.

The use of case scenarios and exercises during the home study will facilitate discussion and the exploration of key issues. The provision of written guidance and access to materials relating to the fostering role, e.g. a foster carers' handbook, foster carer's agreement and safe caring guidelines, will serve to focus on the realities and requirements of the fostering task.

Over coffee and biscuits, she systematically took apart our lives to find out how we operated individually, how we worked as a family, what our past and future hopes were, the state of our finances and how we hoped to cope with the demands of concurrency. She even interviewed our daughter to find out her feelings about a possible adoptive sister or brother. We had warmed to Sara, our social worker, on our first meeting and this proved to be crucial. Neither of us could have opened up in the intimate way we needed to if we hadn't felt a real bond between us...So for us knowing that the questions were asked not from frivolity or bureaucracy but to ensure the safety and happiness of a child made us willing to open up and share details of our lives with a relative stranger. And in return for our honesty, Sara shared her feelings about how the process was going with us. She felt we were doing really well and had dealt with issues in our past and learned from them, which would, if anything, enable us to face the future and the huge demands of concurrency as stronger people.

(Brighton and Hove concurrency adopter)

Loss and uncertainty

The assessing social worker needs to evidence the applicants' capacity to manage and tolerate a sustained period of uncertainty, and potential or actual loss of the child if rehabilitation becomes the plan. It will be important to draw on evidence of the applicants' experience of managing uncertainty and loss, and their resilience to other events in their lives, including information on their current adult functioning. Loss is a very significant factor in any adopter assessment, but it is of additional significance in concurrency when the carers may be exposed to potentially heightened levels of feelings of loss and despair. If adoption becomes the plan, carers may also feel very affected by the loss for the birth parents if they have developed an empathic relationship with them during the fostering phase. Some concurrency adopters also expressed considerable disappointment about not having a relationship with the birth parents, as that was what they had prepared themselves for and they had felt positive about the benefits of direct contact.

> *She turned up once and said she would like to meet us but she disappeared again. It is sad because I feel we have missed out in one sense. And it's the baby's long-term well-being, and we cannot fill those gaps.*

(Concurrency adopter in Monck *et al*, 2003)

It is particularly important in the assessment to consider how couples have worked to support each other through difficult life events and their use of professional and other support systems. Single applicants will need to have access to close confiding friendships within their support network.

Referees and wider family and friends

It may be appropriate for agencies to consider arranging information and support sessions for close family and friends of concurrency applicants or approved carers to help them to make sense of the model and consider the role they could usefully play. The assessing social worker needs to explore the referees' understanding of concurrent planning and views on the applicants' ability to manage the task. It could be helpful to provide prompts about concurrent planning on the proforma that agencies use for reports of referee visits. The meetings with referees will provide evidence of how the applicants have explained concurrent planning to their close family and friends and their decision making about this route.

Prospective adoptive grandparents who may have longed to become active supportive grandparents will need to understand that the child coming into their family is being fostered and may return to their birth family. Discussion has to take place with the applicants about how the concurrency process may be managed by their wider family network and who may be able to provide the kind of support they will need. For example, prospective adoptive grandparents will need to be able to put their own feelings and expectations, hopes and fears on the back burner if they are to play a supportive role through the fostering phase.

Other children in the family

As with all assessments of applicants who are already parents to either birth or adopted children, there needs to be careful consideration of the impact of not only the potential adoption but the fostering phase and the uncertainties of that process on the other child/ren in the family. Applicants need to consider how they will balance meeting the needs of their children with the needs of a fostered child. They need to consider this not just in practical terms, but in terms of how they will address the issues of fostering a child who could potentially become their child's sibling if adoption becomes the plan. Dependent on the age of the child, thought will have to be given to an age-appropriate "script" for the child so they can explain that their family is fostering a child.

The impact on the child already in the family of the potential for the fostered child to be returned to their birth family also needs some careful discussion. There will be particular issues for applicants coming forward as concurrent carers for a birth sibling of their adopted child. Issues relating to their previous experience of contact with the birth parents and the level of contact their adopted child has with the birth family will be a factor for consideration.

If there is an option for applicants to meet or make contact with other experienced concurrency or mainstream adopters who have a family situation similar to their own, this may be of particular value.

The fostering task

The reality of managing the fostering task and the feelings of powerlessness that carers are likely to experience through the concurrency process is also an area that needs particular attention during the assessment. Discussions during the assessment need to focus on considering how the applicants manage feelings of lack of control in everyday situations. For example, prospective concurrent carers may within their professional working lives have a high-profile role with a lot of responsibility and power to make decisions. They are going to have to manage a potentially protracted fostering role and a court process that makes a decision about the child in their care to which they will not be able to contribute.

All prospective adopters have to manage feelings of vulnerability and powerlessness during the application, assessment and matching stage, but for concurrency carers these feelings may be very acute during the fostering phase and will need to be considered and covered within the assessment report.

Contact with experienced foster carers and adopters

If possible, applicants should have the opportunity to have contact with concurrent adopters or foster carers who may have relevant experience of caring for a young baby. The assessing social worker can use material from this contact to facilitate discussions and evidence the applicants' readiness for the task. Applicants who have not had experience of parenting will need to have the opportunity to develop their knowledge and confidence in caring for young babies.

When a baby is placed with first-time carers, they will be caring for that baby under the glare of professional oversight and scrutiny. They may have to manage questions and criticisms about their care of the baby from parents whose own parenting capacity is subject to critical assessment. This scenario is very different to that experienced by mainstream prospective adopters when they have an infant placed in their care for adoption. Concurrency brings another layer of complexity and prospective carers will need to have undertaken sufficient preparation for the realities of the day-to-day caring task during the assessment stage.

Contact

The practical and emotional demands of contact need to be fully addressed. Carers have to be prepared to organise their daily routines around contact and need to consider the implications of this on their family situation. For a couple, it will be important for the carer who is not at home full time to have the opportunity to attend contact on occasions and meet the parents and directly share some of the issues in relation to contact. Having some flexibility with work commitments will be important. Single applicants may need to consider whether there is anyone in their network whom they can use for support around contact. Having the opportunity, for example, to meet up with a friend whilst a contact session is running may be a source of considerable support.

The applicants' capacity to empathise with the parents and have some understanding of the contact experience from their perspective also needs to be considered. The stakes are very high for all parties during the concurrency process and this is acute for the parents during contact. They will be aware that the carers looking after their baby want to adopt the baby if the outcome of the assessment is not positive.

There may be particular issues for lesbian or gay carers about how the birth family may react to them as carers and potential adopters. These issues should be addressed by the assessing social worker and support should be available to all the parties in resolving these issues.

Adoption leave and pay and implications for concurrent carers

It will be important to consider at an early stage within the preparation and assessment phase the practical, financial and employment implications of the concurrency process for the prospective carers. As foster carers, the concurrent carers will receive a fostering allowance from the local authority whilst the child is placed with them on a fostering basis.

Prospective carers will need to make enquiries of their employers of the implications of undertaking a fostering role that may or may not potentially lead to an adoptive placement. All prospective adopters should be given the basic information about statutory adoption leave and pay and advised to inform themselves about the particular policy of their own employers. The situation is more complicated for concurrent carers in a number of respects.

- Concurrent carers may have to leave their employment at very short notice if they are matched with a baby and the court then endorses the concurrent care plan. There is often a need to move quickly to minimise the baby having any delay in being placed with their concurrent carers. Prospective carers need to consider how this may fit with their work situation and decide how and when to discuss the detail and implications of the concurrency task with their employers. Prospective concurrent carers may feel understandably concerned that they do not want to jeopardise their work situation, given the uncertainty of the concurrent fostering role and the possibility that if the placement is made, the baby may go on to be rehabilitated with birth parents within a number of months.

- As foster carers, concurrent carers will not be eligible for adoption leave or pay during the fostering phase. This will commence once the care proceedings have concluded and the adoption match has been approved and a "matching certificate" has been provided by the adoption agency as evidence of the placement. Concurrent carers will need to discuss whether their employers will agree a period of special or unpaid leave to cover the fostering phase of the concurrent placement. Prospective carers will need to consider carefully how they will ensure they have time off work for the fostering phase before any entitlement to adoption leave commences and how they will manage the financial implications of this. Some prospective carers may decide that they wish to resign even though they will be fostering a child who may not go on to adoption. It might be helpful for the agency to provide some written information for prospective carers about this aspect of the concurrency process so that carers are able to consider this and think about the options that they may have in terms of their work situation. This information can also be given to their employers, if appropriate, to help to explain the role they plan to undertake. Within England, the Children and Families Bill 2013 contains provision to consider the leave and pay arrangements for prospective adopters who have looked after children placed with them, so this will have relevance once enacted for concurrent carers.

It has been the experience of the early concurrency teams in England that this did not prove a particular disincentive to prospective carers. Most carers found employers prepared to be flexible to accommodate the fostering phase and provide unpaid leave for this period. Some carers appreciated the fact that if adoption was to become the plan, they would not technically commence their adoption leave until the child had been with them for a number of months and adoption and the match with them had been formally approved. It is very important for carers to understand at an early stage what financial support they will have during the fostering phase, i.e. what the weekly allowance will be and whether there will be any additional payments made for initial equipment or travel to contact, etc. Concurrency foster carers, like all foster carers, need to have access to advice about the tax implications of their fostering allowance and their status as foster carers.

Second opinion reports

Many agencies include a second opinion report by another member of the adoption team or the assessing social worker's supervisor as part of the assessment report. Such a report should comment on the preparation and assessment work undertaken and include an analysis of the applicants' capacity to undertake the concurrency process and their preparation and readiness for the task ahead.

Summary of additional issues to cover within the assessment

- Employment – practical arrangements and capacity for the applicant to leave work, possibly at short notice, and the impact of the fostering phase on future employment. Are the applicants' employers prepared to be flexible about time off for the fostering phase?

- Financial assessment needs to take account of the fostering allowance for the fostering phase and the delay in access to adoption leave or adoption pay.

- Assessment of any relevant health issues, including emotional wellbeing, will need to pay particular attention to how the applicants recognise, understand and manage stress. This needs to be considered for the individual and for the couple relationship if assessing a couple. Carers will have to manage the task of parenting whilst dealing with a high level of uncertainty about the plans for the baby and having their parenting subject to professional scrutiny.

- The applicants' understanding of the fostering task and how they will make use of professional supervision and support. The carers will have to cope with loss of privacy and autonomy to make certain decisions and manage further intrusion into their lives.

- The applicants' understanding of the legal process/the length of court proceedings and the role of others in making assessments and presenting views in court about the eventual outcome. Evidence will be needed of how applicants have managed when they do not feel in control of an aspect of their life. The applicants' capacity to recognise these feelings and strategies they have used in the past will be of relevance.

- The impact on other children within the family of the concurrency process. Dependent on the age of other children in the family, what preparation has been undertaken and consideration given to how the carers will help their child/ren with the level of uncertainty and the fostering task?

- The impact of concurrency and the prolonged uncertainty on other family members and key people within their network and who they will access support from, particularly during the fostering phase. In whom have they chosen to confide about their decision making in relation to concurrency and how have they described this?

- An outline of how the applicants will manage the practical demands of contact and fit this around other responsibilities, e.g. care of other children/school holidays, etc.

- The process of decision making by the applicants in opting for the concurrency route and how their learning and understanding has developed and changed since the application, along with their motivation and understanding of the risks associated with the role. The applicants' capacity to manage and withstand the impact of the potential loss of a child in their care in the context of their fertility/infertility history will need to be fully addressed.

- The capacity of applicants to manage the relationship with the birth family and their understanding of situations that may lead a baby to be placed concurrently.

- How the whole family will manage the changes to their lifestyle during the fostering phase and transition to rehabilitation or adoption. The impact on day-to-day family life and leisure time activities must be considered – it may not be possible, for example, to have family holidays whilst fostering due to the level of contact commitments.

- A description within the analysis and summary of how the applicants expect to combine the roles of foster carer and prospective adopter. How they will cope with the inherent tension of providing a secure attachment relationship for the child whilst working within a framework of care planning that could result in the child returning to the birth family must be considered.

- A consideration of matching issues and management of health and developmental uncertainty. Any experience of caring for babies and any additional learning or experience gained during the assessment phase should be noted. Matching considerations will also have to take into account the needs of older children in the family, as appropriate. This may include, for example, the potential longer term impact on any existing children in the family of developmental uncertainties for the child placed concurrently.

Second-time adopters

Prospective carers may be experienced adopters who wish to consider concurrency as a route to adoption second or even third time around. As with all subsequent assessments of prospective adopters, the focus of the additional assessment is on the process of decision-making for the second time around, their experiences of parenting through adoption and the potential impact on their child/ren of adopting again and any additional support needs or particular matching requirements. Applicants need to have the opportunity for full exploration of all the issues related to the concurrency task, as it will be a very different experience to their previous route to adoption. Even second-time concurrency adopters have to understand that their next experience of concurrency could be unlike their first and have a potentially different outcome.

There will be particular issues for applicants coming forward for the birth sibling of a child they have adopted. They will also need to explore the particular significance for them and their child of fostering a sibling in the knowledge that this child may not remain within their family.

Fostering for adoption carers

As outlined in the introduction to this guide, the Government in England has introduced fostering for adoption (FfA). FfA is intended to complement the existing practice of concurrent planning and potentially extend the number of children in care who can achieve early permanence via adoption.

From 1 July 2013, an amendment to the Care Planning, Placement and Case Review (England) Regulations 2010 enables prospective adopters approved by either local authorities or voluntary adoption agencies to be temporarily approved as foster carers for **a named child** by the local authority with the responsibility for that child (see Regulation 25A of those Regulations). These carers will not have to be approved as foster carers under the Fostering Services (England) Regulations 2011 and will not need to be considered by a fostering panel. Fostering for adoption practice guidance emphasises that information about this potential route to adoption should be included within the adoption agency recruitment material and that prospective FfA carers will need to be carefully prepared and assessed for the task.

> It is important to ensure that carers are fully informed about the nature of the placement, their role in that placement as foster carers and their understanding of the possibility of the court deciding to pursue an alternative plan to adoption.
>
> (Simmonds, 2013)

A report in relation to the prospective adopters evidencing their capacity to undertake the role as local authority foster carers for a named child will have to be prepared. Good practice would suggest that this report should be submitted to the agency decision maker for approval. The agency decision maker will need to be confident that the carers are suitable to undertake this specific fostering task and that they can meet the needs of the child as set out in their care plan. The issues to be covered in the preparation of FfA carers fit with those detailed within the section in this chapter on preparation for concurrent planning carers.

THE PANEL PROCESS

Panels provide an essential source of expertise, continuity and quality assurance and the local structure of panels for concurrent planning will need to be considered to ensure that they are fit for purpose. There may be a number of ways of addressing this depending on local circumstance, but experience suggests that the model of adoption and permanence panels is the most effective. As such, the panel will need to be familiar with the model of concurrent planning including the objectives, advantages, risk factors and outcomes.

The adoption and permanence panel will need to be compliant with the fostering regulations and adoption agencies regulations and make effective use of the central list. It is recognised that this may take some re-adjustment to current structures and the operation of panels. Discussion will need to take place with the legal adviser, agency adviser and agency decision maker to consider any changes needed to the constitution and terms of reference for the panel to enable the panel to make recommendations about the applicants as prospective foster carers and adopters.

The panel will need to ensure that there is sufficient consistency in the panel chairperson and central list members to provide continuity in reviewing the available reports and evidence wherever possible, in considering:

- the suitability of concurrent carers as foster carers in the first instance and as prospective adopters; and

- the match and adoption placement of the child with the prospective adopters (formerly the concurrent carers), if the plan becomes adoption and the court makes a placement order.

The particular nature of these placements, especially in their progress during the fostering phase, provides a level of evidence and detail about the carers' strengths, development and resilience that is unusual when panels typically consider the *potential* of prospective adopters and the *potential* for the match.

It is also important for the agency decision maker, chair and central list panel members to be briefed, trained and supported in the specific issues that might arise in concurrent planning. It is helpful that there are opportunities in the annual appraisal process for central list panel members to reflect upon how this has worked. Briefing will need to take place prior to the first assessments of prospective concurrent carers being presented to the panel. Panel members will need basic familiarisation with the concurrency process and an opportunity to learn about the additional components of the preparation training provided to prospective applicants. Any additional sections or prompts that the agency has made to their assessment framework will need to be provided to panel members so that they have a clear understanding of the expectations of concurrent carers.

There may be occasions where the child is fostered by the concurrent carers for more than 12 months. Should this be the case, the first annual review of the concurrent carers as foster carers will need to be completed and presented to the panel for a recommendation about their continued approval as foster carers.

SUPPORT AND SUPERVISION

The role of the supervising social worker

There are very strong advantages in the concurrent carer being supervised by the same social worker who undertook the home study assessment. If that is not possible, there will need to be a full handover and briefing of all the information available from the assessing social worker. The newly approved concurrent carer needs to feel confident about the level and quality of support they can call on, and the supervising social worker will need to know the carers well and be able to respond with sensitivity and skill to any issues that may emerge during the matching or fostering phase.

The particular demands of concurrency placements should be recognised within the caseload weighting for supervising social workers. The task will involve a high level of responsive visiting, telephone and email contact with the carers, plus availability for support around contact times, particularly in the early stages of the process or if the contact arrangements are being changed in response to the development of circumstances with the birth parents. There may be a need for the supervising social worker to make time for contact with other members of the concurrent carers' family, such as older children in the family, if particular issues emerge during the fostering phase.

The carers will need careful preparation and support for key meetings such as LAC reviews, medical appointments or meetings with the child's social worker or Children's Guardian. The supervising social worker should ensure that they are available to attend meetings with the carer or have time to support them before or after such meetings, as appropriate. All these meetings will have a heightened significance for the concurrent carer over and above that experienced by the professional baby foster carer. Independent Reviewing Officers will need to be fully briefed about concurrent planning prior to undertaking a review meeting of a child placed with concurrent carers. Good preparation for such a meeting is essential and the supervising social worker may have to take a lead role to ensure that the IRO and other parties are fully aware of the status of the placement. The IRO will need to give careful thought to the planning of the meeting to enable the parents and carers to participate appropriately and to ensure issues of confidentiality are not breached.

Out-of-hours service

Most local authority fostering services provide an out-of-hours "on call" service for their foster carers so that they have the reassurance that they can access advice and a listening ear out of normal office hours. This may be particularly important for concurrent carers during the early days of the placement or if the carers are managing a difficult phase of the fostering process, perhaps with a plan for the child to be rehabilitated to birth parents.

Contact with the social worker for the child

The supervising social worker will need to ensure that they retain very close liaison with the social worker for the child so that they are fully briefed on the progress of the assessment of the parents or wider birth family. There will need to be close communication about visiting arrangements, day-to-day care of the child and expectations of the carers. A clear agreement should be in place at the outset of the placement about the working relationship of the social worker for the child and supervising social worker for the carer. This will include how information is shared and the process for both workers to have access to reports of their contact with the carers and the child in placement. The concurrent carers need to understand how the two workers involved in their day-to-day life will work together and how the wellbeing and safety of the baby will be their priority.

Support during initial matching and the move to the concurrent placement

The matching, introduction and transition process will probably take place over a very short period of time for children with a concurrent care plan.

The supervising social worker needs to ensure that their carers have as much information as possible and an opportunity to ask questions and reflect and consider the issues for them in relation to the child.

In some circumstances, carers may be asked to consider a potential match and then the plan for the child may change. This may result from a change in the care plan if, for example, new family members come forward for assessment or a concurrent care plan is not agreed at court. For the carers there will be an intensity of feelings, as they assimilate information about a child who may be their potential adoptive child, plan for the potential placement and are then informed that the plan is not proceeding. Carers will need time to manage the highs and lows of the process and be supported to consider when they are ready to be linked with another child who could be placed concurrently.

If a placement does proceed, the carers need to know in outline what the plan is for the assessment of the parents and what the parents need to achieve to enable them to be considered able to take on the care of the baby. The carers need to know how they will be kept informed of the progress and the various stages of the legal proceedings. Issues relating to matching and decision making about concurrent planning are covered more fully within Chapter 5.

The initial period of the placement may also require particular support as it is often the culmination of a long period of planning, thought and reflection. The shock of finally having a baby placed and having to adjust and respond to caring for a young child, respond to the feelings of other family members and friends and start the arrangements of contact visiting may initially be overwhelming.

One concurrency adopter illustrated the difficulties of managing all the different expectations of them as foster carers but also prospective adopters. She said that some relatives sent them congratulations cards when they first had the baby placed, even though they had explained that they were just fostering the baby initially. She said they felt really embarrassed that they had left the cards on the mantelpiece when their social worker came round to visit.

Another experienced concurrency adopter described the overwhelming feelings of upset and fear that she had when the baby was first placed. She questioned for the first few days whether she could love this very fretful baby or had the ability to care for her properly. She said her partner stepped in and took over and she gradually regained her confidence and developed a close loving bond with the baby over the next few days. She said she was shocked by the strength of her feelings and found her initial reaction something very difficult to share with others at the time as she felt she should have been so excited about the placement of the baby.

(Accounts from Brighton and Hove concurrency adopters)

Some carers may have to manage the fact that the child they are being matched with may have had an extended period in hospital or a period in foster care before the concurrent placement is agreed. An experienced Coram concurrency adopter reflected on that experience:

> It breaks my heart I couldn't be there for him (during the first four weeks in hospital, as the baby was born with neonatal abstinence syndrome) – I still well up thinking about it.

She was also concerned about his early days in foster care:

> At the foster family it was a very busy house, he was passed around, all lovely people, but I feel he found the transition easy (to us) because he was used to being passed around.

Another concurrency adopter reflected back on her experience of having a baby placed from hospital:

> I think Molly had missed the bonding because she was in hospital for three months. That's the crucial thing. That's what I've had to come to terms with really.

Support groups

Consideration should be given to establishing a support group for concurrent carers facilitated by social work staff whilst carers are in the fostering phase. There is considerable value for carers in having the opportunity to access support from their peers, but they will also need to maintain confidentiality about the details of the birth family circumstances. Carers will also be at different stages of the process – some may just have had a baby placed whilst others may be going through a particularly difficult or challenging phase in relation to their contact or the progress of the plans for the baby in their care. It may be difficult for a carer to express their feelings of excitement and relief about their forthcoming adoption plans if they are aware that another carer may be experiencing a very different outcome.

Support needs and contact

There will be particular support needs relating to contact and the impact on day-to-day life for the carers. Experienced concurrency adopters have reflected on contact being one of the most challenging aspects of the task. Concurrent carers will have a perspective on the contact arrangements that will need to be listened to. This may range from how the contact may impact on the day-to-day routine for the baby to the particular needs of the baby in their care. Carers are also likely to have some unforeseen commitments or other demands in their domestic lives that will require a level of flexibility when planning for contact.

A concurrency adopter in Brighton and Hove, recalling her experience, said that 'It helped that I was put in touch with an experienced concurrency adopter who provided an additional level of support as she had been through it herself and could relate to what I was experiencing. I remember her saying: "Don't let yourself get pushed around and make sure you have your voice heard," and this was a helpful message when I was struggling with the impact of contact on the baby as well as meeting the needs of my older child in the family.'

Issues relating to contact and the role of the supervising social worker and support needs for carers are addressed more fully in Chapter 7.

Concurrent carers need to have a listening ear for the difficult or overwhelming feelings that they are likely to experience. The assessment will have focused on how the applicants may support each other or who within their close confiding network can drop everything to come round when needed. Carers should be able to confide in their supervising social worker, but many experienced concurrency adopters have talked about the constraints of this relationship at a time when they felt quite vulnerable about the outcome for the child. Carers talk of having angry feelings at times about the birth parents or finding handover at contact extremely difficult. Carers have to trust that the vulnerable infant they are caring for is going to be safely cared for by the birth parents, even with the presence of the contact supervisor.

> Concurrency carers need more support (practical and emotional) than to be treated only as foster carers during the period of parental assessments because they are being asked to make an emotional investment in loving a child that a professional foster carer never needs to make. We think counselling should be available as a right to every concurrency carer.

> (Brighton and Hove concurrency adopter)

Attachment and bonding

Some carers interviewed as part of the Monck *et al* evaluation (2003) describe anticipating during the assessment phase how they might protect themselves from developing intense feelings about the child during the fostering phase. However, many then describe how this was unrealistic once the baby was placed.

> I don't think we held back during the time we were only fostering him. My other child definitely attached immediately and adored the baby. In my quieter moments I loved the baby just as much and didn't hold back. I think that maybe this was because I thought there was only a minuscule chance of him returning to the parents. Perhaps it would be harder for people who haven't got another child.

> (Adopter in Monck *et al*, 2003)

A Brighton and Hove concurrency adopter described being told very clearly by their social worker that they could only call themselves by their first names when talking to the baby; she said that it soon became very apparent that the birth parent had relapsed into her longstanding drug use and was continually failing to attend contact. She said:

> We did then start referring to ourselves as Mummy Deidre and Daddy Duncan to the baby when the social worker was not present as we wanted to ensure that the baby was not missing out in any way in having a secure loving family.

A concurrent placement provides the opportunity for the baby to experience a close secure attachment relationship and most carers describe developing an intense bond with the child in their care and endeavouring just to remain focused on the day-to-day care needs rather than dwell too much on the uncertainty of the outcome. That attachment relationship also enables the carers to cope with not just the uncertainty of the outcome of the court proceedings, but also to deal with any issues that may emerge in relation to the infant's health and development. The benefits for the child of experiencing such attuned care during the first few weeks and months of life, even if reunification becomes the plan, are significant. The same can also be said for slightly older infants who may be placed with concurrent carers after experiencing neglectful or abusive care within their birth family.

Other professional support

It may be important to consider who else can provide professional support to the concurrent carer. Carers may need access to specialist, independent counselling support if the plans are progressing towards rehabilitation. At such times, it can be very important for carers to have the opportunity to discuss their feelings with someone outside the professional decision-making process. If such a service is to be provided, it will need to be readily available and easily accessible.

A number of experienced concurrency adopters have mentioned the health visitor as playing a particularly significant role in developing a close relationship with the carer by providing a frequent level of oversight and contact with the baby, both as a child in care but also as a baby with a likely higher level of health needs. One Brighton and Hove concurrency adopter said of her health visitor:

> She was my rock; she was so reassuring and gave me confidence in my parenting as well as understanding how I was feeling.

Health professionals can play a critical role but they will need to have full understanding of the concurrency process. Part of the implementation planning must be to give full consideration to how information about the model is provided to other key professionals. The consultant nurse for looked after children could be used to provide additional support and specific advice to health visitors when a local authority is planning the introduction of concurrent planning. The particular role of the medical adviser or consultant paediatrician is covered within Chapter 5.

Foster care reviews and foster carer training

The supervising social worker will need to be mindful of the national minimum standards for fostering and that within England concurrent carers, as foster carers, need to operate within that framework. Chapter 5 gives more information on the implications of this, including the need to ensure that all the appropriate documentation is provided to the carers about the looked after child in their care. As approved foster carers, the supervising social worker needs to ensure that the concurrent carers are subject to an annual fostering review if they are continuing in a fostering role beyond 12 months of their approval. Most concurrent carers are matched with a child within a short timeframe and go on to become adoptive parents within that time, so are unlikely to be subject to such a review.

Some concurrent carers may benefit from attending particular foster carer training courses during the fostering phase, although for many the demands of the concurrency process may not make that easy. Currently, new foster carers in England are expected to complete the training and development standards for foster carers within 12 months of approval. These standards provide a national minimum benchmark that set out what foster carers should know, understand and be able to do within their first year of fostering. Concurrent carers are not embarking on a fostering career and therefore it would not be appropriate or reasonable to expect them to undertake the work to complete these standards. However, this will need to be considered and explained within the agency's foster carer training strategy. Local authorities and VAAs must consider all the implications of the fostering status of concurrent carers. There may be further changes to the regulatory framework for concurrency carers and fostering for adoption carers that recognise the particular role these carers are undertaking and their additional approval as prospective adopters.

Support needs through transition to rehabilitation/adoption

Support needs are likely to be heightened as the local authority plan for the child is finalised and the final care hearing approaches. There has been limited experience of supporting concurrent carers where the plan becomes rehabilitation but a small number do progress to a point where contact is being increased and a rehabilitation plan is becoming a reality. There are also situations where family members who had not come forward at an earlier stage are being assessed as potential permanent carers. In such situations, supervising social workers need to be attuned to the support needs of the carers and proactive in their approach. Carers need regular information and support at meetings to provide updates and to discuss any implications. There needs to be good, ongoing communication between the key staff involved, particularly the social worker for the child and supervising social worker but also with the health visitor and Guardian.

If the plan progresses to rehabilitation, carers may need external counselling support. A plan should be agreed for post-rehabilitation support with agreements made about how any updates on the child's welfare are provided. Agencies should be prepared to provide intense ongoing support and decide with the carers if and when they feel ready to be considered again for a potential adoptive placement. An adoption review, to consider the implications of the outcome of the concurrency placement, would be good practice in these circumstances.

For most carers, even if adoption is the plan, there is likely to be a mix of emotions. Once a placement order has been made in court, carers have described feeling very conflicted: relief and excitement on the one hand, but also empathy for the birth parents and an awareness of the significance of the outcome for the child in their care. All the regular procedures for approving the adoption match will need to be adhered to and the carers may need additional time to adjust to their change of status and changes in parental responsibility, contact and support. One Brighton and Hove concurrency adopter said:

> I felt that my experience during the fostering phase was unlike any other fostering role. You are living with a certain level of anxiety the whole time and I felt I was on hyper-alert during the care proceedings waiting for the outcome to be decided.

Another Coram concurrency adopter said:

> His mother did try very hard to put her life together. She fought as hard as she could to get him back. At one point our Coram social workers told us she had managed to kick heroin and she was clean and that it did look like she stood a good chance of getting him back.

Adoptive families with children placed concurrently are just as likely as mainstream adopters to need access to ongoing adoption support services. Although a concurrent placement mitigates against some of the implications for babies of delay in being placed with a secure permanent family, these are still very vulnerable infants whose health and future development may have been adversely impacted by their experiences in utero, their very early life experiences and also their genetic heritage. Adoption support needs should be assessed in accordance with the statutory framework and a clear plan drawn up about these services, their availability and their expected outcomes.

7

Contact

SETTING THE SCENE

During care proceedings, contact arrangements between infants and very young children and their birth parents or relatives have a central place in concurrent planning practice. Good quality contact can provide the opportunity for parents to learn and practise skills in meeting their child's basic needs. It can provide reassurance to the parents that their child is well and that they remain important to them. Contact can help build and maintain relationships between them. With skilled and consistent contact supervisors, contact allows interactions between parents and their child to be observed, improved and evaluated. However, while contact is a core part of concurrent planning, it is only part of the important work that the parents need to do. They will be required to address the central problems that have led to their child being removed and this will almost certainly be challenging, time-consuming and intensive.

During the assessment phase, it is best practice, wherever possible and safe to do so, for young children to be brought to and collected from contact by their concurrent carers. Such an arrangement provides consistency of care during the journey and the child will not need to adjust to a further caregiver. It also provides an important opportunity for the carers and parents to develop a relationship through handovers at contact. Both parties can use this opportunity to develop a clearer understanding of the people in the child's life, both in the present and for the future, whatever the outcome. If the child is adopted, this relationship lays the foundation for the carers to be able to talk to the child about their birth family as they grow up and for both parties in addressing any arrangements for post-adoption contact. Should the child return to the birth family, their family will be able to provide information and memories about the concurrent carers.

In fostering for adoption placements, careful consideration should be given to the involvement of the FfA carers in contact, and many of the practice points in this chapter will be relevant.

THE IMPACT OF CONTACT ON INFANTS

Contact arrangements have a very significant impact on infants and very young children and it is important to plan the arrangements carefully. The infant has a need to establish a secure attachment with their concurrent carer and they need consistency, continuity and routine to be able to do this. The infant also needs to see their parents or relatives on a regular basis whilst the possibility of rehabilitation is being assessed. However, even with well supported and good quality arrangements, frequent contact visits can be exhausting, disruptive and sometimes very distressing for infants and very young children.

It was very difficult to get the baby into any routine as contact times changed and the assessment involved parents attending at different times of the day for contact. The parents wanted to have every opportunity to feed Arthur and I was told to try not to feed him before contact. But that was very difficult if he appeared hungry – at times I did not feel contact was child-centred enough.

(Brighton and Hove concurrency adopter)

The contact arrangements made it difficult to do anything else like go to a parent and baby group with Alice.

(Brighton and Hove concurrency adopter)

He was deeply upset by contact...he was very, very distressed and this took him months to get over.

(Concurrency adopter, quoted in Monck *et al*, 2003)

RESEARCH FINDINGS

As mentioned in Chapter 2, recent studies on the impact of contact on infants in concurrent planning in England and infants in care in Australia have commented on the stress and distress experienced by young children resulting from contact (Kenrick, 2009; Humphreys and Kiraly, 2011). In her study, Kenrick interviewed 26 former Coram concurrent carers and sought their reflections on their child's experience of contact. She noted that often the children were experiencing contact five times per week, which involved their concurrent carers transporting them to a contact venue which could involve long car journeys or travel on public transport. She provides powerful examples demonstrating the distress experienced, particularly when the child is aged between five and eight months, when separation anxiety becomes apparent. For example:

After two months of three-times-weekly contact at approximately the age of five-and-a-half months, Joe began to become much more distressed during the contact visits. Paula (his concurrent carer) could hear him getting more worked up and crying in quite a different way to any she had ever heard, different in quality. Increasingly his distress could be seen to start as she left the room. She saw the birth mother trying to comfort Joe by jiggling him, she thought much too vigorously, and being unsuccessful. It became the practice, after ten minutes of inconsolable crying, that she would return to the contact room and comfort Joe until he was more relaxed. Then she would leave the room again. When Joe again became more distressed she would have to return. She described her anguish while listening to him crying, wanting to be with him to help him and knowing that she could not go until the agreed time.

Schofield and Simmonds (2011), in their analysis regarding contact arrangements for infants in care proceedings, comment:

The main concern for the infants from this study (Kenrick) was the constant disruption to their daily routine. Unsettled and distressed or shut off and unresponsive infants would be brought back from contact, perhaps settle and recover during the evening, only to set off again the next day. This pattern was rarely limited to a specified period of assessment but continued through proceedings, including where final hearings were delayed. In contrast, on days with no contact it was possible for carers to allow the infant a relaxed day in which feeding, sleeping, play and interaction with carers could allow the infant's natural rhythms – with both physical and psychological benefits.

The potential effects of such early disruptions were still evident for some children after adoption had taken place. This was demonstrated through difficulties in other transitions, i.e. starting play groups or school. For other children, it was thought likely that the attachments formed in the concurrency phase and the close involvement of the concurrent carer in the arrangements alleviated some of these effects.

Humphreys and Kiraly (2011) undertook a larger study in Australia involving 119 infants under one year in age. These children were in short-term foster care during care proceedings, not in concurrent placements. They conducted focus groups with foster carers, practitioners and parents' legal representatives. The researchers reported on concerns raised about the impact on young children of the high frequency of contact, inadequate venues, transportation issues and the involvement of a variety of different escorts and supervisors. Concern was expressed that some children were developing indiscriminate attachment patterns and many had difficulties in feeding, sleeping and showed high levels of distress. The importance of providing therapeutic support during contact visits was emphasised, as was the need for good communication between foster carers and parents. It was felt that much more could be done to improve the quality of experience for the child. A key finding was:

> The pattern of reunification was similar for infants with both high-frequency and lower-frequency family contact arrangements. While further analysis of subsets of the data would be of value to explore this further, it does point to a flaw in the general assumption that high-frequency family contact leads to improved rates of family reunification.

There therefore appears to be no causal link between frequency of contact and reunification; instead, successful rehabilitation tends to be associated with parents' motivation and their determination to make changes before and after the birth of the child. Abstinence from the use of drugs and alcohol and separation from abusive partners and the availability of a range of support services are key components. Humphreys and Kiraly (2011) argue that for contact to work well:

> ...the key focus of work needs to be on supporting quality rather than quantity of family contact for infants in care.

These studies reflect similar concerns that have been expressed by many practitioners and carers across the UK about the impact of very frequent contact on young children. Case law in England has set out a framework that contact between infants and their parents should be reasonably arranged for 'most days of the week and for lengthy periods'. (See Munby's judgement *(Re M (care proceedings: judicial review)* ([2003] EWHC 850 (Admin), [2003] 2 FLR 171). More recently this has been challenged and clarified and a more child-centred approach has begun to be developed.

Further to this, Lord Justice Munby (2010) has now made it clear that the courts should take account of relevant research findings when directing plans for contact (President of Family Division/Family Justice Council debate, December 2010). It is therefore important that the research messages are set out clearly for the court to consider in agreeing appropriate contact arrangements. Relevant information on research findings in neuropsychiatry and brain development can be found in Music (2011). It may also be helpful for social workers to consult an appropriate medical practitioner (neo-natologist, LAC consultant nurse) when considering how contact arrangements can take account of the needs of withdrawing babies or babies with particular special health needs.

Caution is also being expressed, and there are some criticisms of the studies undertaken (see Dale, 2011). Dale expresses concern that the resources needed for intense intervention with birth families could be reduced and, with the current focus on adoption, little work will be undertaken to explore the potential for reunification. He comments that messages setting out that contact arrangements should be less frequent for babies are in danger of being extrapolated for all situations, including older children.

It is important to be clear that the research messages involve vulnerable infants and young children whose parents and families have very significant difficulties. Care planning must take account of individual children in individual situations and offer a fair and reasonable opportunity to the parents. It is the quality of parental interactions with their child during contact that is significant. Schofield and Simmonds (2011) comment:

> ...any "rule of thumb" for contact is inappropriate; rather, the needs of each infant, the circumstances of his or her care, the characteristics of the contact parent and the resources available for contact all have to be considered.

Contact arrangements must be child-centred, well planned and supported and provide a positive experience for both the infant or very young child and the birth parents or relatives.

Infants whose caregivers are sensitive and responsive learn that they are thought about, loved and can readily get their needs met. Because discomfort and anxiety are relieved by their caregivers, babies can pay attention to the world flexibly, being interested in their caregivers and other people, and enjoying the exploration of toys and new experiences.

(Schofield and Beek, 2006)

It is really important to explore with parents how they are able to respond to and meet the needs of their child. Key caregiving dimensions identified by Ainsworth *et al* (1978) are very helpful. These include:

- caregivers or parents who are **available** to the child so they can begin to trust;

- caregivers who **respond sensitively**, thus helping the child to start to manage feelings and behaviour;

- caregivers who **accept the child**, thus building the child's self-esteem; and

- caregivers who provide **co-operative caregiving**, thus helping the child feel effective and autonomous.

(See Schofield and Beek (2006) for further reading.)

Fahlberg (1994) points out the importance of seeing whether the parents are aware of the baby as a separate individual with her or his own needs. She suggests a number of areas that should be considered in making an assessment about attachment levels. These areas can be observed during contact sessions and include whether the parent:

- responds to the infant's vocalisations;

- changes voice tone when talking to or about the baby;

- engages in face-to-face contact;

- encourages age-appropriate development;

- responds to the child's cues;

- comforts the baby;

- enjoys close physical contact;

- initiates positive interactions; and

- can identify positive qualities in the child.

The following indicators (Katz *et al*, 1994) are also useful.

- The parent shows empathy for the child.

- The parent responds appropriately to the child's verbal and non-verbal signals.

- The parent has an ability to put the child's needs ahead of her/his own.

- The child shows comfort in the parent's presence.

- The parent shows an ability to ensure the child's safety.

MAKING INFANT-CENTRED CONTACT PLANS

- **The purpose of contact** It is essential to be clear about the purpose of contact. When the plan is exploration of the possibility of rehabilitation, the primary purpose of contact is to enable the parents or other birth family members to retain or establish a relationship with the infant or very young child. Contact therefore provides key opportunities for parents to learn and practise basic parenting skills and time to enjoy being with their baby and for their baby to be with them. Contact arrangements need to facilitate this and frequency alone cannot achieve this. It is what happens within contact sessions that matters. There should therefore be a plan that maximises the opportunity for good quality contact where the parents also have sufficient time and access to appropriate services outside of contact to address the issues that have prevented them from providing their child with a safe and loving home. This means being realistic about what can be accomplished within such time and resources so that the parent has the emotional energy and focus to think about their child during the visit. Emotional attunement and sensitivity are the key components of parenting during the early years and these should be the focus during the contact sessions.

  It should be noted that even where contact sessions go well, this may not result in the return of the child if the parent is refusing to undertake or successfully complete other required objectives. The role that contact plays as one objective and one part of the assessment therefore must be made clear.

They all led me up the garden path, everyone, you know. They said, 'You have got such good records with seeing your baby'. I have never let them down about seeing her, well, one contact I missed but that was the flippin' bus services. So everything was fine, you know, everyone said how well I'd done in everything but it obviously just wasn't enough.

(Birth parent quoted in Monck *et al*, 2003)

Other relatives may be involved with the parents in a supporting role and some occasional contact will enable the formation of a relationship with the infant. There should be caution about involving too many other family members because of the consequences for the child and the importance of maintaining a primary focus of contact with the parents. The involvement of others should be included in initial contact agreements and kept under review.

- **The infant or very young child's needs and circumstances** At the heart of the plan must be consideration of the infant's needs for a secure attachment and predictable routines. Contact cannot replicate the experience of 24-hour care by highly attuned and sensitive carers who are providing a secure base for the child. Contact has the potential to disrupt this secure base and will need to be carefully managed by parents, carers and supervisors.

  Any vulnerabilities of the child will need to be taken into account, for example, if the child is born with neonatal abstinence syndrome.

Babies with neonatal abstinence syndrome merit caution and care when arranging contact as the person administering the prescribed medication needs to be very familiar with the baby's individual behaviours. Subtle changes have to be noted, which could indicate a need for adjustment to the timing or amount of the dose. Contact must be arranged to fit with the medication schedule, rather than attempt to train other care workers or the contact supervisor to give the medication. The main carer needs to be the person giving the regular dose. The medication is usually morphine or a similar sedative and both under- and over-dosage can have serious consequences for the baby. The baby is often fretful and sensitive, finding changes in routine very uncomfortable and she or he can be particularly sensitive to touch or changes in temperature. She or he can also be slow and difficult to feed and these issues should be taken into account when arranging the time, venue and circumstances for the contact sessions. Withdrawal programmes from medication for these babies vary in length depending upon the severity of withdrawal symptoms, but they can continue for three months or so.

(Vanessa Wright, former Looked After Children Consultant Nurse, Brighton and Hove, November 2012)

If the child is assessed as likely to be suffering from foetal alcohol spectrum disorder or foetal alcohol effects (see Chapter 5), then this will also need to be planned for depending on how the symptoms manifest themselves. Similar plans will need to be made to ensure that the child's care is the primary focus of arrangements made for contact.

- **Settling-in time** When the concurrent placement plan is agreed, the infant or very young child will move to their concurrent carer either from their parents or family, hospital or from another foster carer. For some children, this separation will result in mourning the loss of previous carers. In addition, some children will have suffered abuse or neglect and a range of other adverse experiences. Research and good practice indicate that they will need a period of time, at least a few days, to settle into their new placement with their concurrent carers without undue disturbance before the first contact visit is arranged and takes place or is restarted.

- **The individual needs of the parents and other family members** For contact to be meaningful and work well, it is very important that the needs and circumstances of the parents and birth family have been fully assessed. Parents will be facing a number of major challenges in addressing the issues that have prevented them from being suitable parents to their child, including alcohol and/or drug misuse, mental illness, learning difficulties and domestic violence. There may also be other impairments that impact on their daily functioning. Any of these may result in a range of vulnerabilities and this will include many feelings about their child being removed from their care and the possibility of them being removed permanently. They will also be faced with engaging with treatment programmes and arranging practical issues such as housing and finance. There may be other people in their lives who pose particular dangers and they will need to end those relationships. There may also be particular cultural and language needs that must be taken into account. Within all of these considerations, the parents will need to be helped to plan their travel arrangements to and from contact. They will need to be supported to think through what they can realistically expect from contact and what they might feel about their child and meeting their child's carers. They will need to think about who they can turn to in managing their emotions at times where the infant shows a clear preference for the concurrent carer.

  > ...it was hard for us both because we turned up there and she (the baby) kept crying all the time, she didn't want to know me and her dad. She wanted X (the concurrency carer).

  > (Birth mother quoted in Monck et al, 2003)

- **The involvement of concurrent carers** Wherever possible, they will be required to transport the infant or very young child to and from contact. They will be unable to do this if there is any assessed risk to their safety, e.g. a parent or relative has threatened violence or shown a

111

determination to find their address. Consideration will need to be given to how they will travel and over what distance, bearing in mind the needs of infants and very young children. Good practice and the experience of the English projects suggest that a 20-mile radius is usually realistic but the actual travel time will need careful consideration. Concurrent carers may also need to be available to be brought back to the contact centre early should the infant require this and they should be prepared for this. They will also need to consider what they do whilst the contact visit is taking place. It can be particularly painful for concurrent carers when and if they hear the infant's distress when being left for contact. Their care will be scrutinised by the parents and they may feel personally criticised. Opportunities to debrief and be supported will be needed.

> *In my experience the parents were quite combative – they felt that the baby should have started on solids and were at times very critical of my care. I needed a lot of support from my social worker and sometimes it felt that the workers were just focused on ensuring the birth parents felt listened to.*
>
> (Brighton and Hove concurrency adopter)

> *I particularly valued the support I had from my health visitor. The parents were critical of the homemade food I brought to contact for the baby. The health visitor helped me work out how to manage this issue effectively with the parents.*
>
> (Brighton and Hove concurrency adopter)

It can be helpful for concurrent carers to share some of the contact commitments with their partner (if a couple).

> *It felt good to be able to share the contact commitments with my partner at times and also helpful for them to meet the birth parents.*
>
> (Brighton and Hove concurrency adopter)

- **Handovers of the infant or very young child at contact** Concurrent carers will usually be required to undertake handovers with the parents at the contact venue, and they therefore need to be prepared for what can be an emotionally stressful event for all parties. Concurrent carers will often be asked to exchange information with the parents about the progress of the child and convey this in a sensitive way. They will need to be able to keep diaries about the child for the parents to read. The parents may also want to contribute to the diary commenting on what has taken place during contact. These diaries can be an important component of life story material for the child.

> *Initially I was terrified of upsetting the parents and getting something wrong in their eyes. I was always thinking about what I said and how I said it.*
>
> (Brighton and Hove concurrency adopter)

I didn't like giving him back to them (the concurrency carer) *at the end of contact. Also he used to look round the room for them, not me. But I like "X" and "X". They're honest with me. They keep a diary of his sleeping, feeding, when he first went out in the car seat and so on. They showed me his diary whenever we had contact.*

(Birth parent quoted in Monck *et al*, 2003)

- **The frequency and length of contact** As already stated, each contact plan should be tailored to each infant's needs and research and practice experience should inform this. There should be close liaison between the child's social worker, the carer's social worker and local authority lawyer in considering the most appropriate plan. Contact sessions should be held at the same times and on the same days, wherever possible, and this may need to change in line with the child's changing developmental needs and the progress of the assessment work. The emphasis must be on the quality of contact from the child's perspective. It is also important not to set up parents to fail by aiming for an unrealistic number of contact sessions which they cannot sustain. They will want to prove they are reliable and committed wherever possible.

- **Venue** The venue for contact is very important, and it needs to become a safe, accessible and familiar environment with a welcoming and comfortable atmosphere and an appropriate range of facilities, including age-appropriate toys. There should be facilities for preparing and heating food and making bottles as required, along with facilities for changing and bathing the child. Workers need to be available to greet people as they arrive. The contact supervisor should be on site to facilitate the handovers of the child and be present during the session itself.

- **Transportation** Usually the child's concurrent carer will be expected to transport the infant or very young child to and from contact. If this is not possible, an escort, preferably the contact supervisor, will need to be arranged. This person should be introduced to the child beforehand and should remain a consistent escort throughout travel arrangements.

- **Contact supervision** The role and function of the contact supervisor is fundamental to contact working most effectively. Continuity and consistency of supervisor are key components and it is important that the supervisor's involvement in contact is an active one. They are there to maintain safety and observe interactions but they are also there to facilitate a good experience for the child. Contact supervisors therefore need the skills, knowledge and authority to undertake this important task. They need to be fully knowledgeable about infant and child development and child care, possibly with an NNEB qualification or NVQ. They also need foundation knowledge of attachment theory.

Contact supervisors must have great skills in diplomacy and a calm but assertive approach as they may need to prompt parents to respond sensitively to the child's cues. Doing this in a respectful way that enables rather than undermines is very important in such an artificial environment. Modelling how to feed, bathe, sing, play games and recite nursery rhymes may be required. They also need to be clear regarding professional boundaries, and to intervene and end contact if necessary. Training and good supervision for them will be required.

It is essential that contact agreements are explicit for everyone about the development of parenting skills for parents and how these will be practised and supervised during contact. Some parents will need a programme of parenting skills work before they can be expected to demonstrate their ability to undertake basic tasks and anticipate the needs of their child within a supervised contact. Some parents may have significant learning difficulties or a learning disability and parenting skills development programmes and expectations within contact sessions will need to be tailored to these. Contact supervisors should be absolutely clear about their role and the parameters of supervision required.

It is important that contact supervisors provide feedback to carers too.

> *We would have liked more information from the contact supervisor about exactly what had happened in contact and how the baby had been. I was sometimes just told that a session 'had been all fine' and later on when adoption became the plan and I read the whole file there was a lot of information on the recordings of contact that I would have liked to have known at the time.*
>
> (Brighton and Hove concurrency adopter)

There may not be time for full feedback to the carers at the end of contact and the supervising social worker should have oversight of the carers' experience of contact and ensure that they have the opportunity to receive and give feedback about the experience for the baby. It may be helpful for the contact supervisor to visit the carers and the baby at home to observe the baby in the care environment.

- **Recording and reports about contact** The contact supervisor will need to make notes during the contact sessions as appropriate and prepare regular reports on contact. The contact agreement should detail how contact will be recorded and how parents will be provided with access to these reports. Any issues should be flagged up clearly and immediately so that learning opportunities can be maximised. The finished reports should be factual and reflect the noted careful observations. The contact supervisor may be asked to provide an evaluation in a separate section and all recordings should be completed within a few days and sent to the child's social worker. The parents should be given the opportunity to read these and make comment. There also need to be regular review meetings with the child's social worker and the parents about the progress of the work.

- **Feedback forms** should be provided to parents and other relatives so that they can give feedback on a weekly basis if they wish. Any comments should be taken seriously and criticism dealt with transparently and courteously.

- **Contact agreements** The key contact arrangements will be agreed in court and the above practice points may help in defining those arrangements. A working contact agreement should then be drawn up and agreed by all parties. The agreement should set out detailed expectations and ground rules. For example, it should explain who is allowed to attend contact, the timings, the taking of photos and situations where contact will not take place, e.g. should the parent arrive under the influence of drugs or alcohol. It should be made clear that workers assessing the parents and the Children's Guardian may also attend sessions as part of their work and that the parents will be informed beforehand about such arrangements. The review of contact arrangements and the timescale for this will also need to be agreed. Again, parents should be reassured that they will have the chance to comment on these (see Appendix 5).

CONTACT IN PRACTICE

First contacts

It is really important that the responsible social worker facilitates a face-to-face meeting between the parents and concurrent carers prior to the first contact visit. Parents can be encouraged to ask questions about the concurrent carers and vice versa.

I asked about them and their family and if they have got any pets, and how big is the house, and have they got a garden, and how strong is their marriage...you know, things like that.

(Birth parent quoted in Monck *et al*, 2003)

They asked me how I was and about my other children. They showed an interest in me, unlike a lot of other people.

(Birth parent quoted in Monck *et al*, 2003)

The contact agreement will need to be drawn up with the parents and everyone should have the opportunity to meet workers and the contact supervisor before contact.

Parents should be invited to visit the contact venue beforehand if possible to familiarise themselves with the facilities and equipment available. Concurrent carers may wish to do this too if they are not familiar with the venue. It may be helpful to collect and bring the parents to their first contact session and any practical concerns in relation to travelling to the contact venue should be addressed at the outset. After this, usually they would be expected to travel by themselves, with public transport passes or financial support provided if required. They may need the provision of a taxi for several weeks in some circumstances, e.g. if the mother has had a caesarean section.

Handovers

As already stated, the handovers between concurrent carers and parents and birth family members need careful planning. Wherever possible, if there are two concurrent carers caring for a child, it is hoped that both will be present for the first meeting with the parents. It is essential to maintain the confidentiality of the concurrent carers and only first names should be used. It is important to avoid giving away details of addresses or other identifying information.

Workers need to ensure as far as possible that the parents and concurrent carers do not meet inadvertently when contact is being arranged, for example, it is important to be alert to the possibility of parents and carers arriving simultaneously at the venue's car park. It may be that the concurrent carers' car needs to be parked elsewhere. It is therefore good practice to ask the parents or relatives to arrive at contact some time before the session. The contact supervisor can greet them and take them to the contact room to look at any reports about the previous session, make any comments they may have and discuss other issues of concern. The parents may also wish to have the time to prepare the contact room and set out any toys or equipment they wish to use. This may enable the parent to feel more empowered if they are taking some responsibility for the contact preparation.

When the concurrent carers and child arrive, they should be met by another worker who can take them to a waiting area. The contact supervisor should then come and accompany them and the child to the contact room. The carers should update the family on the child's progress such as the child's feeding patterns and when they last fed, their toileting and changing, sleeping, games and any other issues of relevance. The carers should bring a bag with a favourite toy, nappies, drinks, bibs, dummy (if used), creams, extra clothes, etc. It is probably easier if the carer keeps a bag specifically for contact and ensures that it does not contain any identifying information.

The concurrent carer will be expected to use a contact book or diary. This will record important changes and progress for the child, e.g. that he or she is now sleeping through the night. It is helpful to advise the parents on any activities the baby or young child particularly enjoys. It is also important to ask the parent for their views and preferences regarding the child, e.g. whether they would be happy for the carer to take the child swimming.

In most cases, concurrent carers and parents are anxious about each other at the beginning of the arrangements but with support and careful planning, the potential for them to develop a warm and respectful relationship is very possible. The handovers usually should take no longer than 10 minutes.

I made a note of any information I gleaned from the birth parents during handovers. I found out things they liked and this has all been useful information that I have been able to provide for my child now.

I valued contact with the parents. I felt I got to know them as people after reading reports about them.

I felt a range of emotions about the birth mother. Before I had really got to know her I felt quite angry with her as the baby was very unsettled and fretful as he was born addicted. I then did get to know her through contact and felt guilty when the plan became adoption...she slid back into heroin use but I know after such a longstanding habit it had been so difficult for her to stay clean.

Generally it was a good experience but sometimes the parents didn't turn up or had to be asked to leave when they did arrive as they were under the influence of drugs. I sometimes felt worried about leaving Cal as I was aware that the mother would get sleepy in contact. I did feel reassured by the presence of the contact supervisor. Generally the mother managed well and I was aware that she felt very embarrassed about her drug problem. She was really open and honest and approachable. I used to keep a diary between contact visits so I would have something to say and felt prepared to talk about Cal's sleeping or eating or whatever he has been doing.

(Comments from Brighton and Hove concurrency adopters)

It is important that the carers are contactable in case they need to return early. On some occasions, the concurrent carer may need to stay in the building or for the whole session if the child is judged to need this.

Contact sessions

Coram's information for concurrent carers sets out:

It is for the supervisor, link worker and parent to plan for contact. In the contact room, the mother or father can feed, change or bathe the baby. Parents bring food, and sometimes store toys (a locker should be provided), and clothing. It might be that the parent would wish to be the first to give a baby solids. Depending on the circumstances, there may be opportunities for parents to go out with the supervisor for a walk, or to local groups, such as Surestart.

Tips from an experienced contact supervisor

Make things clear from the start

- Remind parents what concurrent planning is, the point of being here, the two plans. Remind them that part of the supervisor's role is to work with parents to help them and give them the best possible chance of having their child returned to their care. For example, I usually say: 'None of us is perfect, we can all learn, baby care practice and advice changes all the time...It's my job to let you know areas that could be improved, things that you could do differently. If I didn't do that I wouldn't be being fair to you or doing my job properly.'

- Make sure that parents know you will be writing contact reports that describe what happens in contact.

- As the placement progresses, you may need to keep reminding parents of what you told them at the beginning.

Suggestions or giving prompts

- You may need to make suggestions about how to do something more appropriately. The tone of voice you use is important so that you don't come across in a confrontational or coercive way. For example, I might say to a parent who is finding it hard to feed or soothe their baby: 'How I find it helps to do this is by doing...', or: 'You might find this an easier way of holding the baby so that you are supporting her head...'

- There are times when a parent may have picked up the baby's cues but does not know what to do. For example, they have picked up that the baby is tired but do not know what to do to help the baby settle to sleep. I might say: 'I think you are right, G is tired...What can we do to help him settle to sleep? Maybe if we make the room a bit quieter or turn the lights down.'

- If the baby is distressed and the parent is unable to calm him or her despite your suggestions, ask permission to try and settle the baby. I might say: 'Sometimes a different person can help to settle an upset baby'. If the parent does not want you to take the baby but the baby continues to be distressed, I continue to be inclusive but also more directive: 'Let's see if she's happier if I walk her round the room for a few minutes'.

- For a parent who is interacting with or stimulating a child in an appropriate way, I comment on this and praise them, saying why it is important: 'Babies really like to be able to see your face and hear your voice...and another thing you could think of doing is...'

- Something you have given advice about previously may crop up again. For example, you have previously advised a parent to wash their hands after changing a nappy. I don't always remind the parent the next time they start changing a nappy because that doesn't give them an opportunity to show they have remembered. I will only prompt again if necessary.

Pre-empting conflict between birth parents and concurrent carer

- There is the potential for conflict at LAC reviews or medicals where concurrent carers and parents are present. I find that who answers the health questions and gives information can be difficult issues. I therefore talk to both carers and parents separately ahead of these meetings, acknowledging that it might be difficult and thinking ahead about how they might feel. For example, I would suggest to a parent who is inclined to fly off the handle that the best way to be listened to is to stay calm. Even if they feel angry, shouting and swearing won't help.

The report

- Helpful suggestions, advice and reminders about baby care matters that have been discussed during contact do not get in the way of a useful and fair report; the report will make it plain that the parent was not able to calm the baby without help and support, or that they were about to pick the baby up without washing their hands after nappy changing although that has been discussed several times previously. It will also make it plain if they did retain and act on advice.

(Comments by Coram contact supervisor, November 2012)

The involvement of parents in parenting or other family support groups will need careful consideration. It may be difficult for the parent to attend particular groups as these may not be local to where he or she lives. Where these are being considered, careful thought needs to be given to the involvement of the contact supervisor and explanation, if needed, of their role to others.

It is important that the contact supervisor takes photos during the sessions for life story purposes if necessary, and this will have been set out as part of the contact agreement. Two albums should be made so that the parents have their own copy if reunification does not become the plan.

We have lots of photos of the birth parents with Felix at contact and also photos of us with the birth parents – in the future I think this will be really helpful.

(Brighton and Hove concurrency adopter)

My daughter likes looking at the photos from contact – these are very important to her.

(Brighton and Hove concurrency adopter)

Ending sessions

At the end of the contact session, the contact supervisor will take the child back to the carers while the parents or birth family wait in the contact room. The supervisor will need to give the concurrent carer any information regarding the child's feeding, bathing, or nappy changing or any other matters of relevance to their care. The concurrent carer and the child will then leave the venue. The supervisor will return to the parents to discuss their experiences of the contact session and make any plans for the next session. Once the parents or family have left, the supervisor can in turn be debriefed.

Feedback from carers and parents

It is important that the concurrent carers can speak to their supervising social worker about the impact of contact on the child and discuss any anxieties that they may be experiencing. It is equally important that the parent and birth family members can also give feedback about their experience of contact. These are highly intense and emotional meetings for everyone. Any concerns should be listened to and addressed, as appropriate.

Immediate feedback from workers to parents

Workers should provide clear and honest feedback to the parents about how contact is progressing. If parents do not attend or are late, workers must address this with them immediately. In some cases, the parents will need reminding of the importance of their attendance at contact and their need to undertake agreed work, given the very high stakes involved in achieving reunification or adoption. Katz (1999) commented on the importance of making vigorous efforts to promote parental contact even with ambivalent or unresponsive parents:

> The agency's zeal in promoting visiting (contact) would result in either faster reunification or early decision making in favour of an alternative plan.

Reviews

It is important that contact reviews take place regularly and involve social workers, the parents and the contact supervisor. Regular feedback can be given about progress and difficulties. Arrangements will need to increase if rehabilitation appears a likely outcome or they will reduce significantly should adoption become the agreed plan.

CONTACT AND SUPPORT SHOULD REHABILITATION BE THE OUTCOME

In cases where the rehabilitation plan is working well and the parents or birth family member are making the required changes to enable them to care safely and appropriately for the child, the contact arrangements will be reviewed and will need to become more frequent. In such cases, contact will change to take place in the parent or birth family member's home and eventually become unsupervised. A planned return will take place where this is agreed by the local authority and the court.

In these cases, the concurrent carers and the parents will need a very intense level of support and it is essential that workers' time is available so that they can offer this. Those workers who have been involved with the carers and parents during the assessment phase are often best placed to offer this support, although independent counselling may also be offered. Workers will need to continue to be present for every handover and contact between carer and parents. This gives the message that no party is alone and everyone remains clear about the plan and what is going to happen. Workers need to be available at any time over the reunification period and the out of hours service for foster carers should be alerted to the potential need to provide additional contact and support to the carers, as required.

Rehabilitations through concurrency can be isolating for concurrent carers who may feel set apart from other carers who have gone on to adopt their children. In one example at Coram, the parent wanted to be sensitive to the carers' loss but also wished to celebrate. The carers felt they had to pull away from other concurrent carers who often found the situation too anxiety-provoking. The carers lost not only the child but their support network of other concurrent carers.

CONTACT AND SUPPORT SHOULD ADOPTION BE THE OUTCOME

In many cases, the seriousness of the parents' and birth families' difficulties will rule out rehabilitation despite every effort being made to achieve this. Assessments will have been undertaken and it will be agreed that adoption by the concurrent carer is now the plan. The contact arrangements will therefore need to be reviewed in line with assessments and agreed within the court proceedings. It is likely that contact will reduce gradually and, in many cases, direct contact will eventually end. This is clearly a very sad time for birth family members. In some cases, a parent may be completely opposed to the plan for adoption.

The birth father was vehemently opposed to adoption and had to be removed from a contact session by the police. The legacy of that experience has been quite difficult to process.

(Brighton and Hove concurrency adopter)

It is very important to arrange appropriate farewell contacts. Coram's concurrency planning project organises a "Family Day" which the parents, relatives, concurrent carers and the child attend along with workers. This is planned as an occasion where parents and carers are encouraged to say positive things about how each other have contributed to the child's life. Photos are taken and the parents are given a photo album. Usually two or three weeks later, a separate farewell contact takes place for the parents and the child, facilitated by the contact supervisor. The concurrent carers are often invited to join this contact about 20 minutes before the end.

In some cases, the parents may be able to support the plan, no matter how painful:

It felt very real that Stephanie would return to her birth mother. She had started to look so much better at contact, she left her partner and had got a job and turned up to every contact. However, then it all fell apart for her. She did manage to be very positive in contact and gave her permission for us to adopt Stephanie. She wrote a beautiful letter for her and I feel this experience has helped us have more of an understanding of her and be better placed to help our daughter in the future.

Farewell contacts are often very emotional:

After the final contact, I just walked round for the rest of the day and kept bursting into tears.

I needed to be on my own initially but on reflection maybe a quick phone call from my social worker in the evening would have been good. I then had a proper debrief when the dust had settled.

(Comments from Brighton and Hove concurrency adopters)

Supervising social workers and social workers for the child need to take responsibility for considering the particular support needs of parents and carers following a farewell contact. Parents will often feel an acute sense of loss and will need to be encouraged and supported to access appropriate independent counselling and support services.

CONTACT AFTER ADOPTION

After adoption, contact plans will need to be made. These will need to be very carefully considered as they may be drawn up when people have not yet thought through the implications of long-term arrangements. Concurrent carers can feel guilty that the birth parents are no longer able to see the child. Birth parents and relatives are grieving. Although people may have worked well together in contact during the fostering phase, direct contact arrangements for children over time can be particularly complex. The Good Practice Guide *Planning for Contact in Permanent Placements* (Adams, 2012) offers helpful practice points in assessing what contact plans should be considered.

Whatever plans are being drawn up, the child's needs must be at the centre. Key questions will include: how will contact benefit the child in terms of identity and continuing relationships? What are the birth parents' feelings towards the child's adoption? Will they support the adoption or undermine it? What are the views of the concurrent carers about contact? What support will people need? How will any required changes to contact arrangements be flagged up and resolved?

Practice experience by the concurrency projects in England has found that direct contact arrangements have been made more often than for mainstream adoptions. Where planned, these usually occur once or twice a year and in most cases, these arrangements have continued. However, all parties need good support and the arrangements may need to stop and sometimes restart at different times in the child's life. Experience has shown that, in a number of cases where direct contact has been arranged, it often works well for the first few years whilst the child is very young. However, by school age, contact can become more difficult as the child begins to understand the significance of the relationships. Direct contact arrangements are therefore likely to require the active involvement of a contact supervisor over many years. It is important that, from the outset, it is made clear that contact arrangements will be reviewed regularly to ensure that they continue to be in the child's best interests. In most cases, indirect contact will be arranged and practice experience demonstrates that this can be successfully maintained. Again, good support will be necessary.

8

Implementation issues

This chapter focuses on the issues involved in assessing the viability of concurrent planning, decision making about models of delivery and the process of implementation of concurrent planning as a care planning option.

Chapter 3 detailed the background to the concurrent planning model in the US and the early work undertaken in England to establish specialist concurrent planning teams built on the principles of the US model. These discrete teams, based in both local authority fostering and adoption services and VAAs, undertook both aspects of the work. They recruited, assessed, supervised and supported concurrent carers, and also undertook the parenting assessment with parents and the wider birth family and prepared specialist assessment reports within care proceedings. The local authority teams took over the key worker role for the child once the concurrent care plan had been agreed in court.

Different models of delivery are now being developed with the same aim of achieving a speedier resolution of permanence for infants in the care system; these are discussed later in this chapter.

When considering the introduction of concurrent planning into local practice, local authorities and VAAs will need to undertake an analysis of the benefits, challenges and risks associated with providing such a service, taking into account the particular profile of families and children at risk of care, or with plans for adoption, in their area. Consideration should then be given to the different potential models of delivery. The possibility of collaboration with other agencies to develop or buy into an existing scheme could also be explored.

It is essential that a lead senior manager is identified to develop a project plan to consider the appropriateness and viability of the model within their area and then to steer an implementation plan once an agreed model for delivery has been decided upon. Accessing the perspectives of key senior managers will be essential and a small working group may need to be convened to facilitate this.

Once a decision has been made to implement concurrent planning, this working group can expand to become a steering group to oversee the development and operation of the scheme.

ASSESSING VIABILITY

Collection and analysis of key data

An important starting point for local authorities is an analysis of key data in relation to children who could be placed concurrently, particularly infants under two years of age. This data should include:

- the age and number of children adopted in the last five years;

- the age of these children on entering care and at the time of making an adoption plan;

- the time taken from the agency decision maker's decision for adoption as the plan, to matching with potential adopters;

- the number of children under two subject to a plan for adoption where separation was agreed at initiation of care proceedings;

- the profile of the children (aged under two and subject to a plan for adoption) in terms of ethnicity, geographical location and whether the children are part of a sibling group.

These data can then be used to identify the potential size of the cohort of children who could be placed concurrently.

Care planning pathway

Local authorities will need to consider their system for the early identification of children who could be placed concurrently. This will focus on the pre-birth referral and assessment pathway, the role of family group conferences and the pre-proceedings phase of the public law outline (PLO), and the processes for tracking permanence plans for children subject to care proceedings. Local authorities will vary in terms of how parenting assessment work is undertaken, whether pre-birth or post-birth, and the extent to which specialist internal or external professionals are used to undertake such assessments. A systemic approach to early permanence planning is essential as well as the need to maintain a sense of urgency as the child progresses through the local authority care system. See Chapter 5 for more detailed information on the care planning pathway.

Key stakeholders

Preliminary viability work will need to involve consultation and briefing with key stakeholders. For local authorities, this must include not just senior social work managers, including the Independent Reviewing Officer manager, but also the senior lawyer, the medical adviser(s) and other appropriate senior medical staff. Early discussion needs to take place with the local judiciary and CAFCASS manager through local Family Justice Group meetings or other appropriate legal and court user forums.

The concurrent planning model should be fully explained as there are often misconceptions about the term. A focus on key internal and external stakeholders is essential. It is also critical to take account of the fact that most social work and adoption teams are working under considerable pressure and financial constraint. There may be uncertainty about the potential for concurrent planning, the ethics of the model or just a lack of capacity to consider new ways of working. Adoption practice in England has been under intense scrutiny with significant changes to the guidance and regulatory framework in recent years, and any plans to consider the development of a new working model need to take account of this.

Concurrent planning will not be successfully implemented unless there is a sustained commitment and belief in the benefits of the model from key senior managers within the agency. There will inevitably be doubts and sometimes potential opposition. Managers and staff involved in delivering the model will need to be confident and passionate about the benefits to vulnerable children in the care system. Potential concurrent carers will only opt for involvement in this route to adoption if they can fully understand the process and the child-centred principles behind the scheme, as well as having confidence in the staff involved and the support they will receive to manage such a challenging task.

Collaboration between local authorities and the role of VAAs

Consideration of the potential for concurrent planning may usefully take place in adoption consortia. The importance of placing children locally with concurrent carers is a critical issue. Babies and young infants cannot be subject to a long travelling time to contact and therefore carers should be recruited from within a reasonable radius of any contact centre that the parents will be attending.

There may be the potential for collaboration between local authorities and/or VAAs in the provision of concurrent carers. Implementation planning should include consideration of potential models of delivery and, in particular, how contact and parenting assessment work will be undertaken. Consideration could also be given to developing a pilot in one area and procedures for keeping this scheme under review and evaluation so that decisions can be made about rolling out the model more widely within an authority.

Financial considerations

Implementation planning needs to include careful consideration of the potential financial benefits of the model. Concurrent carers will be paid a fostering allowance during the fostering phase, but if adoption is agreed as the care plan at the final hearing and a placement order is made, the foster carers then become prospective adoptive parents and in most situations would no longer receive a fostering allowance. The concurrency process therefore reduces the length of time that fostering allowances are paid, and in most situations would reflect a saving for the authority. In some cases, continued or occasional financial support will be required under the adoption support regulations.

However, there will be additional set-up costs involved in the early development and planning stage. Sufficient lead-in time must also be factored in as the development stage is likely to take at least 12 months before placements can be made. There will be variable financial implications dependent on the model of delivery.

MODELS OF DELIVERY

Once the assessment of local viability of the model has been completed, the next stage is to consider the different models of delivering concurrent planning.

The early teams in England all set up specialist teams which reflected experience in the US. The specialist team model enabled a very focused approach to developing and implementing this new way of working. However, there is now a considerable depth of experience in operating concurrent planning both within a local authority setting and within VAAs.

A number of local authorities are currently developing concurrent planning and are exploring how the model can operate within their existing structures. The drive for adopting this model of working is primarily coming from adoption team managers who are focusing on ways of minimising delay in achieving permanence for infants who are likely to require adoption. In some agencies, a lead social work practitioner from within the adoption team is being identified to take on a development role as well as to undertake the first assessments and supervision of concurrent carers. As more experience is gained in running concurrent planning, these local authorities are likely to consider how the model can be rolled out more broadly and into mainstream practice. It is important that specialist knowledge is not just held with one or two practitioners as this can leave the scheme vulnerable if there are staff changes. Some VAAs are also aiming to implement concurrent planning and are offering a flexible range of services, including the provision of parenting assessments.

Some other local authorities are considering pilot schemes in particular geographical areas. As part of the development work, they are reviewing the local care planning pathway and ensuring that work processes can be flexible to ensure that social work responsibility for work with the child and family is not transferred at a critical point in the assessment and decision-making process. The use of a pilot area enables close collaboration between lead managers from children in need or children in care teams as well as the lead adoption manager. Decision making about geographical proximity of families and carers and appropriate contact centres also needs to be factored into the planning.

The specialist team model

The specialist team model involves recruitment of experienced social work staff who are confident and able to undertake parenting assessments within a care proceedings framework, and are also able to undertake assessments of prospective concurrent carers and take on the requirements of the supervising social worker role. This may require newly-appointed staff to have the opportunity for induction and training in specific aspects of the role, as many social workers may not have had recent experience of both aspects of the work. Within the two original local authority teams in Brighton and Hove and Kent, the emphasis was placed on recruiting staff who were experienced in care proceedings work and providing additional training in aspects of the fostering and adoption work. Both of these teams ran as small fieldwork teams but were managed within the adoption service by an experienced adoption manager. See Chapter 3 for more detailed information on the background to specialist teams.

It is helpful to consider the potential advantages and challenges of this specialist team model.

Advantages

- Provides concentrated dedicated staff time to develop and maintain the profile of concurrent planning as a model.

- Enables staff time to be ring-fenced and protected for this specialist role so staff can respond quickly and flexibly to consider potential referrals.

- Enables staff to undertake both aspects of the work and develop understanding, experience and confidence in working with both birth families and concurrent carers.

- Enables greater flexibility in local authorities for staff within the team to undertake pre-birth assessment work and co-work with fieldwork colleagues prior to a care plan for concurrency being agreed.

- Provides potential for local authorities to purchase the whole package from a VAA, including possible provision of specialist parenting assessment and provision of supervised contact when a VAA concurrent carer is used.

- Enables intensity of support to be provided to concurrent carers and for concurrent carers to develop a relationship with all members of the specialist team.

- Enables ease of close communication between the worker undertaking the assessment of the birth parents, the worker supervising contact and the worker supervising the carers.

- Enables dedicated contact provision for infants placed concurrently, with continuity of the staff involved.

Challenges
- A specialist team may be too small to be viable if there are staff shortages, staff absences or funding constraints.

- A specialist team may not be sufficiently integrated within mainstream services.

- There could be a negative impact on staff of working solely with birth families where the loss of their birth child is a very likely outcome.

- There could be a negative impact on staff of such close involvement with both aspects of the work and a consequent effect on their ability to remain focused on their specific role in each case.

- There needs to be an ability to recruit staff who are able to work confidently with both birth families and concurrent carers.

- Considerable development time is needed to set up a discrete specialist team.

- The high profile nature of the work and the pressures that a specialist team may be under, due to their size, and external scrutiny may impact on team cohesiveness and effective functioning.

Small specialist or project teams also bring their own complexities. Haynes describes one aspect of a project team that may have relevance to a specialist concurrent planning team:

> Professionals may view special projects with suspicion, seeing them as taking away important resources and having the luxury to avoid day to day front-line responsibilities.

(Haynes, 2003)

The scrutiny of the performance of the specialist team can bring its own demands but also its own motivators, as workers can have a greater sense of ownership and commitment. Team members of such small dedicated teams must have a thorough understanding of their individual roles and responsibilities, but also the self-awareness to understand how their behaviour impacts on the group dynamics and effective working of the team. The nature and demands of the work and the need to maintain close communication between team members also requires sufficient experienced management time.

Flexible models of delivery

More flexible ways of developing and embedding the concurrency model are now emerging. The team at Coram in central London – the only specialist team remaining from the original pioneering teams set up in England in the late 1990s – is now offering a more flexible range of services to local authorities and in many situations does not undertake the parenting assessment itself when a child is placed with a Coram family. Coram has worked to set up concurrent planning within local authority teams in Harrow and Cambridgeshire and is supporting the development in a number of other agencies and local authorities through a subscription scheme.

Brighton and Hove has retained its commitment to concurrent planning and has maintained a depth of specialist expertise in this area. The authority has continued to place a few babies each year with concurrent carers since the specialist team was closed in 2009. Some of these babies have been siblings of children who have already been adopted by carers who have been as assessed as concurrent carers second time around. In essence, concurrent planning has been integrated into mainstream working and is actively considered for babies where adoption is a very clear potential care plan. All adoption social workers undertake assessments of prospective concurrent carers, and managers who play a lead role in oversight of family finding and tracking of permanence planning are able to consider the potential for concurrent planning, where appropriate. Supervising social workers for concurrent carers take on a very proactive role to ensure that there is close communication with the social worker for the child so that the carers are kept updated about the progress in care proceedings and are provided with a high level of support.

Both Brighton and Hove and Coram have been able to build on their specialist experience to maintain the potential for concurrent planning by developing a more integrated mainstream approach or through offering a more flexible range of services to local authorities.

Other authorities have used the model to provide the opportunity for the benefit of an early placement with carers able to offer adoption, if that becomes the plan. These include South Tyneside, which has developed this model of working in an incremental way since 2004. This approach to early permanence planning was driven by staff in the adoption team, who were increasingly concerned about the number of young children where the prognosis for rehabilitation was very poor due to the chronic and longstanding nature of the family's difficulties and the significant delays in achieving permanence via adoption for these vulnerable infants.

South Tyneside Council has used this model of planning since 2004. It has obviously only been able to be used with a select cohort of children: children who have had a sibling placed for adoption quite recently and thus there has been no opportunity for positive change in the birth family; children from families who are known to the directorate and are judged to have no commitment to their children; or children whose parents have entrenched addictions to drugs and/or alcohol. From 2004–2011, 12 children have been the subjects of a concurrent plan.

This is obviously a small sample but it is 12 children who would otherwise have had to wait until they were several months old before being cared for by their permanent carers and may have suffered the trauma of being removed from their foster carers. As there are no increased costs in operating such a process, then it is justified, no matter how small the sample is.

In the seven years that the process has been used, there have been a couple of years where no children have been placed in this way and other years where several have. This number represents eight per cent of the children who were adopted during that time. On average, as a small local authority, we have 26 children adopted each year; this in turn represents approximately 12 per cent of the looked after population.

In all of the cases, the plan has concluded with an adoption order.

The benefits achieved have been:

- The child is placed immediately with their adopters once the placement order is granted.

- The child is cared for by their primary carer virtually from birth.

- There are no placement moves for the child.

- The best opportunity for establishing healthy attachments is provided.

- We have seen a child born prematurely reach their milestones much quicker than a sibling who was also born prematurely. The sibling was placed with the same adopters but following the traditional route of an interim placement in foster care before moving to her permanent family.

- Birth parents appear to be more positive about such a placement as they realise the child will not have to move to another family.

- Such placements mean that an extra burden is not placed on our over-stretched fostering services as a mainstream placement is not required.

- Adopters have the opportunity of receiving a very young child into their family.

We have had no formal evaluation of this work, but informal feedback from social workers, adopters, guardians, panel members and adoption officers is that this is good practice that operates to meet the best interests of children.

It should be noted that all 12 placements where we have used this form of concurrent planning have resulted in adoption, and thus a positive outcome for both the child and the adopters. Informal feedback from the carers has all been extremely positive. Although a number have indicated that the period during which they are acting as foster carers is very stressful, due to anxiety that the child might have to leave them if rehabilitation is assessed as viable, they would all say that the benefits of bonding with the child from birth and the joy of seeing the child reach their milestones fully outweigh this.

(Extract from C4EO website www.c4eo.org.uk (The Centre for Excellence and Outcomes in Children and Young People's Services))

Devon County Council also worked to establish a concurrent planning service and used the experience gained from other concurrency teams. Devon, like South Tyneside, decided not to set up a specialist team but instead had lead concurrency practitioners from within the adoption and fostering teams. The project was overseen by the adoption manager and was set up in 2006. Four placements were made in the early years of the project and of those, three children went on to adoption and one returned to their birth family. The loss of key staff caused the project to fall into abeyance; however, Devon is now reviewing practice and considering ways of reviving concurrency as a care planning option.

The virtual or integrated model

Dependent on the size of the local authority, there may be options for initially developing concurrent planning as a pilot in one area. The "virtual team" model involves identification of key managers and social workers from within fieldwork and adoption services who will take a lead role in the respective aspects of the work.

If a specialist team is not set up, there must be clear procedures in place about identification of potential referrals. There needs to be consistency in the key worker for the child, ideally from the pre-birth assessment or initiation of care proceedings to the conclusion of care proceedings with either a plan for rehabilitation to the birth family or adoption.

Key issues to consider for the virtual or integrated model of delivery include the following.

- There is a need for committed and dedicated senior lead managers, ideally from both fieldwork and adoption. These managers must maintain oversight of the development, implementation and running of the model, ensuring the profile of concurrency is sustained and key stakeholders are fully briefed.

- There is a need for processes relating to concurrent planning to be embedded in policy and procedures, and processes for identifying referrals, tracking outcomes and reviewing and reporting on the work to be in place.

- There is a need for social workers involved in the recruitment, assessment and supervision of concurrent carers to be confident in the model and to have sufficient time allocated within their caseload weighting to provide intensive and responsive support to carers, particularly during the matching and fostering phases.

- There is a need for contact to be managed well for the child but also for workers to take into account the particular complexities of the concurrent placement. If carers are to be involved in handover meetings with parents, there must be an intensive level of consistent support provided to all parties to manage this relationship effectively and to ensure the safety and wellbeing of the child.

- There is a need for clear agreements about the respective responsibilities of the social worker for the child, the supervising social worker for the carer and the worker supervising contact. The carers and parents need to understand this agreement. The respective managers for the social workers must maintain close oversight and set up arrangements for regular meetings to review progress, as appropriate.

Particular challenges may include the following.

- Difficulties in ring-fencing dedicated time for social workers undertaking either aspect of the work. This may result in problems recruiting concurrent carers. There may also be difficulties if there is a lack of confidence in the capacity to ensure care proceedings are managed effectively and efficiently, in the capacity for contact to be managed well for all parties, and in the capacity for a responsive level of support to be provided to the parents and carers.

- Ensuring that referrals are identified in a timely way and there is effective oversight of the appropriateness of concurrent planning, i.e. sufficient assessment has been undertaken to determine that adoption is a clear potential outcome, initial viability work with any potential family and friends carers has taken place and it has been concluded that there is no one appropriate or able to offer a short-term placement for the child.

- Maintaining the principles of the model, in particular, ensuring openness and honesty with all parties, explaining in the care plan to court that the fostering placement is with concurrent carers and ensuring there is no drift in the planning and that parents are offered the appropriate resources to develop their parenting skills, as required.

Cambridgeshire County Council, which has a partnership arrangement with Coram, has undertaken development work to set up a concurrent planning service.

Cambridgeshire County Council in partnership with Coram

Cambridgeshire recently restructured its children's social care services to create small social work units providing services to children and families across the county. Each unit has a consultant social worker, two social workers, a clinician (usually a psychologist) and a unit co-ordinator.

Cambridgeshire is developing concurrent planning within its new structure, headed up by the County Adoption Manager who leads the Coram/Cambridgeshire partnership. A steering group involving key stakeholders has been meeting regularly over the past year and there is commitment to concurrent planning throughout the organisation and across key agencies, including the judiciary. A significant amount of training and consultation has been provided by Coram across agencies and with key staff. This has helped to maintain momentum and allowed any early concerns to be allayed and difficulties resolved. Protocols and information leaflets have been developed.

A permanence social work unit has been set up with a specific focus on assessments of vulnerable unborn babies and relinquished babies. From these assessments, the unit identifies children who are in need of concurrent carers and retains responsibility for those children throughout care proceedings to rehabilitation or adoption. The unit then works closely with the adoption service which assesses and supports prospective concurrent carers. Applicants are presented to Cambridgeshire's adoption and permanence panel for a recommendation for approval as both foster carers and adopters. Once concurrent placements are made, there is close liaison with the county's supervised contact service where a specialist contact supervisor takes the lead on supervising contact in concurrent planning situations. Should a child's plan become adoption and the court grants a placement order, Cambridgeshire's adoption and permanence panel considers the proposed adoption match and makes a recommendation to the agency for approval, as appropriate.

(Barbro Loader, Coram/Cambridgeshire Adoption Partnership, January 2013)

Lancashire County Council is also at the early stages of developing their concurrent planning scheme, which was established through an "invest to save" initiative in Lancashire.

Concurrent planning in Lancashire County Council

Lancashire established a concurrent planning initiative in January 2012. It currently has one dedicated social worker who takes the lead in undertaking the assessment, support and supervision of prospective concurrent carers and promoting the model. The project is running initially for three years with a target of placing 15 children aged under two years during that time. (In August 2011 there were 1,335 children in care in Lancashire, which included 77 infants aged under one year.)

There has been considerable work undertaken to promote concurrent planning and to train and inform a range of different stakeholders, including the local judiciary and legal community.

Currently, as Lancashire is developing a pool of carers, the social work teams are informed about carers who may be available to enable consideration of potential referrals. Protocols are being developed in relation to early identification of referrals. Supervised contact is undertaken by the child and parenting support service and concurrent carers are expected to have a role in transporting children to contact, meeting birth parents at handover and completing a contact diary.

It is early days for this new service but one baby has already been placed and there are other prospective carers going through the recruitment and assessment process.

Experience in Lancashire to date has highlighted the importance of:

- ensuring active engagement with key stakeholders to develop understanding of concurrent planning as a care planning option;

- profiling concurrent planning as part of a recruitment strategy and ensuring foster care recruitment also gives a focus to this role.

Challenges include:

- ensuring that all social workers dealing with enquiries from prospective carers are able to discuss the concurrent planning task with confidence;

- managing the issue of carers needing to have agreed time off work as they are not initially eligible for adoption leave, and providing adequate fostering allowances to enable them to undertake the fostering task;

- ensuring that the additional tasks associated with the supervising social worker role in relation to concurrent placements up to the point of either rehabilitation or adoption order are reflected in the worker's caseload weighting.

(Catrina Dickens, concurrent planning social worker, Lancashire Council Council, February 2013)

Voluntary adoption agencies

Voluntary adoption agencies may wish to consider expanding their recruitment to include concurrent carers if there is potential for such carers to be used by local authorities in their area. Such an expansion in recruitment would need to be agreed in local partnership arrangements with local authorities that want to develop or enhance their capacity to place children concurrently. VAAs would have to consider the implications of also becoming a registered fostering agency to enable them to recruit, assess and supervise foster carers.

A VAA would need to develop a range of services in addition to the recruitment, assessment, supervision and support of a concurrent carer. The provision of specialist contact services for infants placed concurrently is an important component of the service available to local authorities and would provide concurrent carers recruited through the VAA with the confidence that staff familiar to them would be available to oversee the contact arrangements. VAAs may also wish to explore the option of providing additional services to local authorities as part of a concurrent planning package; this could include parenting skills, advice work and specialist parenting assessment work.

Barnardo's is currently developing a concurrent planning service in north-east England and has received some consultation and support from Coram with the initial planning.

Barnardo's Fostering and Adoption North East Concurrency Service

Barnardo's Fostering and Adoption North East began work to set up a concurrent planning service in April 2012.

The team undertakes recruitment, assessment and training (carers attend adoption training with additional concurrency training) and offers support after placement. Workers are experienced in both fostering and adoption and carers are able to access ongoing foster care training as well as specialist support if needed. The team has a psychologist specialising in attachment who is able to offer training and one-to-one counselling for the carers, as appropriate. The adoption panel is set up to enable the approval of concurrent carers as both foster carers and adopters.

Barnardo's has a range of services for children and families which are managed separately from fostering and adoption. A parenting assessment worker and worker with responsibility for contact and provision of support to birth parents have been recruited. There is also a dedicated contact room available.

The service has taken longer to set up than initially thought. Early challenges have been the recruitment of carers and identifying local authorities willing to use the service. For Barnardo's, as a voluntary agency covering the whole of the north east, the wide geographical area has also presented challenges.

Various recruitment methods have been tried, including the local newspaper, website and radio and there have been some early difficulties recruiting sufficient carers. For some people, the risk of losing the child has not been something they wanted to consider. Others have been concerned about the financial consequences and the risk of taking unpaid leave from their employment for the fostering phase. There are now three concurrent carers in assessment (going to panel in May 2013), with another two possible carers in the process.

One authority in the local consortium has now agreed a partnership arrangement with Barnardo's. As part of that, Barnardo's staff will attend that local authority's information evenings to promote concurrency as an option and will then take on responsibility for assessment of any prospective carers. That local authority would have priority for placements with those carers once approved.

(Carol Norcott, concurrent planning social worker,
Barnardo's Fostering and Adoption North East, January 2013)

IMPLEMENTATION

Steering group

Once a decision has been made about a concurrent planning service, whether as a discrete team or not, an implementation plan will be needed. All the early teams within England set up steering groups of key stakeholders to oversee the early period of implementation and operation of the team. There are likely to be benefits in maintaining a steering group even after a scheme is well established. The steering group can continue to have a role in maintaining a high profile for early permanence work, support the need for ongoing training and enable the schemes to remain responsive to changes in local need or changes in the statutory framework.

If a working group has been operating during the assessment of viability phase, the remit of that group could be extended to become a steering group for implementation. Group membership and terms of reference may need to be expanded and the accountability and reporting requirements of the group agreed.

In the early days of implementation, it may be helpful for the lead managers to have reference to the steering group to assist in delivery of training and induction and to provide support and advice, given the challenges of establishing a new working model. There may be frustrations about the lead-in time needed before children can start to be placed and the wider steering group could play an important role in maintaining oversight of the implementation work. Aspects of the work will need particular attention, such as ensuring that all agencies involved are clear about how they will maintain confidentiality about the carers, and this could be considered within the steering group.

It is essential to keep the role and remit of the group under review to ensure the work of the group continues to be of value. Steering groups can be important forums for problem solving as well as celebrating successes.

Training

Information and training materials on the concurrency model should be developed as part of the implementation planning. This should include information for birth parents, training and materials for carers, and information and training for social work staff and other professionals. These information materials should be kept updated and training sessions provided at regular intervals for new staff as well as refresher training for existing staff.

Specific material is needed for prospective carers as part of recruitment literature, but information leaflets should also be provided for parents (see Appendices 3 and 4 for examples). These leaflets should give a clear explanation about the process and principles of concurrent planning and expectations of the carers and parents. Social workers should ensure that these are also provided to lawyers representing birth families.

Information booklets for other professionals are also useful; such material should be kept updated and include reference to any relevant research or evaluation of the model. This information can be provided to Children's Guardians, lawyers, health visitors and midwives as well as to social workers.

Brighton and Hove produced a comprehensive *Handbook for Professionals* which included information on the theoretical underpinnings and principles of the concurrency model, referral process, legal framework and processes for assessment of birth parents, the role of contact and the recruitment of carers. This handbook also included information written by concurrency adopters and a birth parent about their experiences.

Evaluation and review

The implementation plan must include a process and timescale for evaluation and review. The early teams in England had the benefit of external evaluation via the Coram research team and oversight of the progress of the teams was part of the role of the steering groups. It is helpful to determine from the outset key data to collect to inform the analysis of the performance of the concurrency model. Any analysis will need to take account of the need for sufficient lead-in time before children can start to be placed.

Data to collect would include:

- the number and profile of infants referred for a concurrent placement;

- the number and profile of children aged under two with a plan for adoption;

- a record of any reason why infants referred were not placed concurrently;

- the outcomes of concurrent care plans;

- the time taken between placement and determination of the final hearing;

- the time taken between the final hearing and the adoption order for those with a plan for adoption;

- a comparison of timescales between children placed concurrently and those placed via the normal fostering and adoption route.

For VAAs, other information to collect could include details of which authorities had used concurrent placements and the type of service used.

As well as quantitative data, there would also be value in establishing a process for collecting and recording qualitative feedback. This could include the views of concurrency adopters post-adoption order about all aspects of the process, including their preparation and support as well as their views on the contact arrangements. It would also be very valuable to collect views from birth parents, if at all possible, and other professional stakeholders.

This information can be used to provide a regular report on the role concurrent planning is playing in the local authority's early permanence strategy or VAA's strategic plan.

Confidentiality

Processes for maintaining confidentiality in relation to the concurrent carers will be critical and detailed thought should be given to this at an early stage in the planning. This will need to involve input from key professionals, including health and legal professionals. Constructing a written protocol in relation to confidentiality is advisable and this could be undertaken by considering every stage of the process and the potential for accidental disclosure of information. Local authorities will need to ensure that concurrent carers are afforded the same confidentiality as adoptive parents on any local authority database.

Consideration of safety and risk issues will be part of the linking and matching process and particular strategies may need to be deployed in relation to maintaining confidentiality dependent on individual circumstances.

The consequences of accidental disclosure of information in relation to the full name or address of concurrent carers can have profound consequences. There have been situations of carers deciding to move house with financial support from the local authority after their full name and location was disclosed in, for example, an expert report within care proceedings. Carers themselves need to be reminded to be very careful not to pass on identifying information accidentally and to rehearse how they are going to introduce themselves at meetings where the parents are present. Attention to detail is required, with supervising social workers taking the lead in ensuring that carers do not pass on any disclosing information at handover times at contact.

9 Conclusion

There have been considerable changes and developments in fostering and adoption practice since the early work was undertaken to establish concurrent planning teams in England in the late 1990s. Currently, there is significant focus by central Government on working to reduce delay in achieving permanence for the youngest children in the care system. Concurrent planning as a model for family placement for infants under two years fits with this imperative.

There is a much clearer understanding now about the impact of delay on young children and the effects on babies of trauma, separation and lack of a consistent, attuned caregiver. The baby's experience of interaction with her or his primary caregiver helps to develop the growing brain and neglect, loss and disruption can lead to developmental problems and delay. Infants who require care away from their birth family have usually already been exposed to harmful pre- and post-natal experiences. The often prolonged uncertainty of care proceedings and potential change of temporary foster carer is clearly not conducive to the needs of infants. Concurrent planning can minimise the impact of this process by creating a more secure, stable and sensitive environment for the infant whilst important decisions are being made about their future.

Also, important research has now been undertaken into decision making about very young children who are likely to suffer from abuse and neglect (Ward *et al*, 2012). Ward *et al*'s study highlights not just the consequences of delay in intervening and removing a child from an abusive family, but also the subsequent disruption experienced by a vulnerable infant when they are moved from a temporary foster carer to a permanent adoptive placement.

This greater awareness about the needs of young infants in the care system and an understanding about babies' timescales for decision making are reflected in central Government policy on adoption and child care planning. There is currently much wider support for the child-centred principles of the concurrent planning approach, with many more local authorities and VAAs now actively exploring the potential for developing this model of work.

There are significant lessons to be learnt from the experiences of the early teams in England, as well as from practice in the US where concurrent planning was originally developed.

Concurrent planning has the potential to help shift the child welfare system towards a model in which permanency – along with safety – is emphasised from the first moment a child enters care.

(Frame *et al*, 2006)

As a model, concurrent planning will need to become embedded within the culture of the adoption agency, whether it is a local authority or VAA. A focus on early permanence will need to be high on all local authority agendas and implementing concurrent planning will require professional, cultural and procedural changes. Formal systems will have to be introduced to support concurrent planning, with local authorities considering their practice in relation to pre-birth assessments and early identification of children who could benefit from a concurrent placement.

This guide has emphasised the need for careful planning, close involvement of key staff including appropriate external stakeholders, building in sufficient lead-in time and developing ongoing training for the range of different staff involved. For concurrent planning to be successful, there has to be an emphasis on strong leadership from key managers and a real commitment to and belief in the principles and values of the model. Experience to date in both the US and UK teams has demonstrated that there can be resistance, doubts and confusion about the model and there may well be challenges and setbacks for agencies. However, there is now considerable momentum behind the wider development of concurrent planning as a care planning option and a clearer understanding that concurrent planning, in essence, represents good child-centred social work practice.

Appendix 1
Brighton and Hove City Council concurrent planning data – for children placed concurrently 2000–2012

Brighton and Hove was the first local authority to develop a concurrent planning scheme, in 1999, with the first concurrent planning placements being made in 2000 within 12 months of setting up the specialist team. The team was managed within the adoption service and remained in operation as a specialist unit until 2009. The team recruited and supervised concurrent carers, undertook parenting assessments within the framework of court proceedings, and also undertook pre-birth assessments in relation to children who were potentially at risk of care proceedings at birth. A number of these children remained with their parents on a child protection plan or within the wider birth family. The team took on key work responsibility for the child once a concurrent care plan was agreed in court and provided a dedicated parenting support and contact service.

Since 2009, the adoption service has retained a commitment to concurrent planning and the recruitment, assessment, supervision and support of carers is undertaken by social work staff within the adoption and permanence service. Brighton and Hove has continued to place a few infants concurrently each year but with key work responsibility for the care proceedings work remaining within the fieldwork units.

From 2000–2012, 61 children were placed concurrently and all went on to be adopted. An analysis of the data on timescales for children placed concurrently highlights the speed in resolution of permanence plans for these infants. Brighton and Hove has concentrated on concurrent placements for infants aged under two years.

All the children who were adopted through concurrent planning met the current Department for Education national adoption scorecard target (Department for Education, 2012e). The scorecard indicator measures the average time it takes for a child who goes on to be adopted from entering care to moving in with their adoptive family. The target for this is currently 21 months, and seven months from placement order to match with the adoptive family. For children placed concurrently, they were all living with their prospective adopters on a fostering basis prior to conclusion of care proceedings.

Figure 1 depicts the age of children at placement, with a significant number being placed directly from hospital. A number of infants were born suffering from neo-natal abstinence syndrome or other additional health needs that necessitated a period of time in a special care baby unit before they were ready to be discharged to foster care.

Figure 1: Age at placement

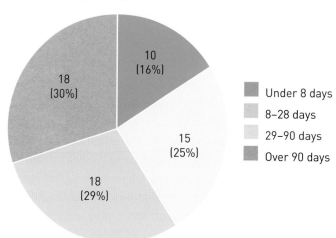

Figure 2 demonstrates the time taken from the date of placement to the resolution of care proceedings and making of the care order. Care proceedings in relation to 34 of the 61 children placed concurrently (56 per cent) were resolved within six months of placement and 85 per cent within nine months of placement.

Figure 2: Placement to care order

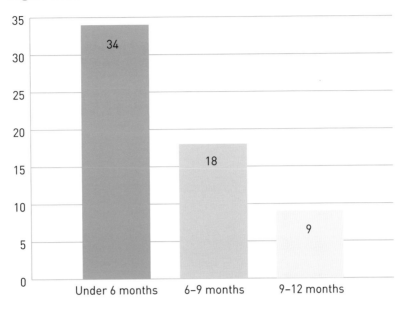

Figure 3 demonstrates the time taken from the date of placement to the making of the adoption order. A total of 47 of the 61 children (77 per cent) were adopted within 12 months of placement.

Figure 3: Placement to adoption order

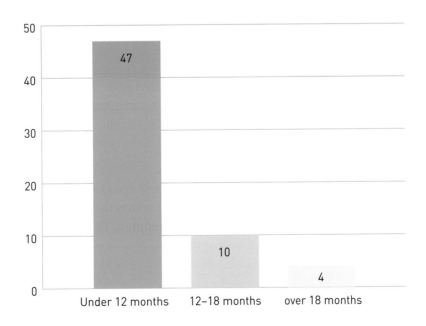

(These data have been reproduced with the kind permission of Brighton and Hove City Council.)

Appendix 2
Coram Concurrent Planning Service: outcomes and timescales

OUTLINE OF WORK

Coram is the only specialist centre for concurrent planning practice in the UK. It has been active in the field for 13 years, and is undertaking a study to examine the social, emotional and educational outcomes for the children who have reached permanency through the scheme. The information reported here draws on the records Coram has kept for all the children placed through concurrent planning; the more detailed study that is underway will further consider the outcomes for 28 children whose parents consented to involvement in the study.

Alongside this research, Coram is developing practical approaches to the challenge of improving performance nationally in relation to early permanency. It is therefore acting as a national centre to assist local authorities and voluntary adoption agencies in improving outcomes for children by offering management services, analytical and practice development support.

Over the life of the project, 57 children had been fostered in concurrent planning foster placements, of whom three returned to the care of a family member, and 54 were adopted. The eldest children are now 12.

KEY FINDINGS SO FAR

Permanency outcomes

The Coram Concurrent Planning Service works actively to enable birth families to take up one last chance of demonstrating that they can care for their child safely. Consistent with this aim:

- three (five per cent) of the 57 children for whom a decision had been made have been reunified with birth families. One child returned to his mother and two were returned to kin carers.

- nationally, it has been estimated that about eight per cent of children placed with concurrent planning carers by the four projects operating up to 2010 had returned home to their birth families (Laws *et al*, 2012).

- for those children not reunited, they continued their placements with Coram concurrent planning carers. A total of 52 (91 per cent) of these children have been adopted by their carer/s to date.

Below are a series of figures representing the children's referral to the Coram Concurrent Planning Service, including children's ages at the point of referral (including if this was pre- or post-birth). The permanency outcomes are also highlighted.

Location of children prior to referral

Once entering the care system, 39 children (68 per cent) whose referral led to a placement spent some time with foster carers and/or relatives before being placed with their concurrent carer/s (the two children who spent time with relatives and in foster care were referred post-birth, see figure below). A total of 18 (32 per cent) were placed with their concurrent carer/s straight from hospital, with the majority of infants (16) being referred pre-birth.

Figure 1: Location of children prior to referral

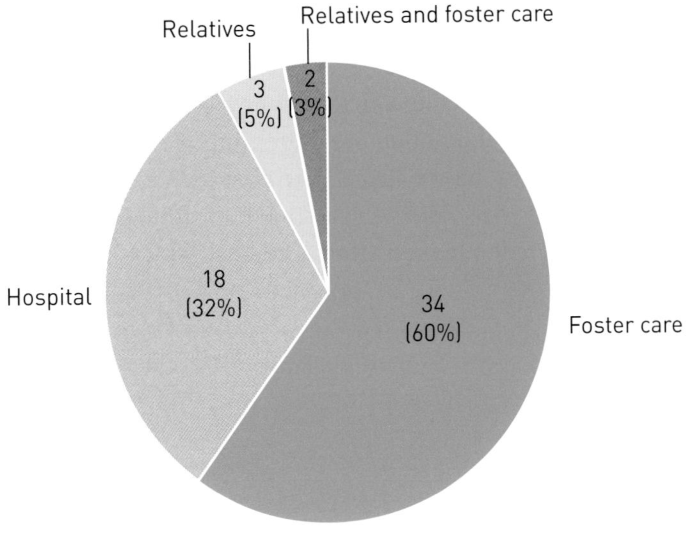

Source: Coram data (2000–2011); n = 57

Percentage of pre-, post- and at-birth referrals

A key aim of the Coram Concurrent Planning Service is to achieve early permanency for children identified as at high risk early in their lives – this means that children can be referred prior to birth, and this is encouraged by the service. Indeed, as shown in the figure below, of the referrals that progressed, pre- and at-birth referrals accounted for 60 per cent (34) of cases.

Figure 2: Percentage of pre-, post- and at-birth referrals

At birth
2
(4%)

Post-birth
23
(40%)

32
(56%)
Pre-birth

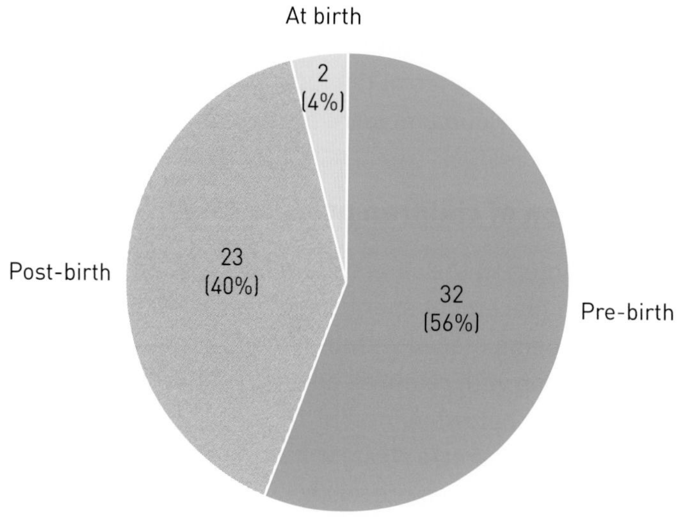

Source: Coram data (2000–2011)

Age of children at referral to the Coram Concurrent Planning Service

A total of 96 per cent of referrals that progressed to a placement were made prior to a child's first birthday. Nationally, only six per cent of the looked after population are under one year (DfE, 2012e). However, it is also true that nationally, 63 per cent of those adopted in 2008–2012 were under one year old when starting their final period of care (continuous period of being looked after) (DfE, 2012e).

Figure 3: Age of child at referral

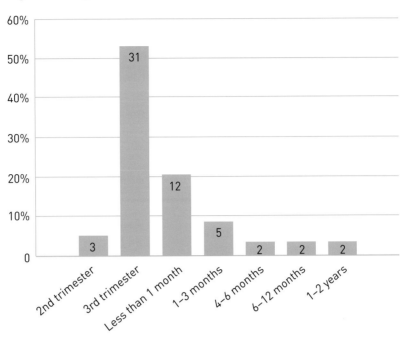

Source: Coram data (2000-2011); n=57

Where child was placed from, by age at referral

Sixteen children who were first placed with foster carers were referred to the Coram Concurrent Planning Service pre-birth, two post-birth and 16 at birth. All children who spent time with relatives and/or foster carers were referred post-birth.

Figure 4: Where child was placed from, by age at referral

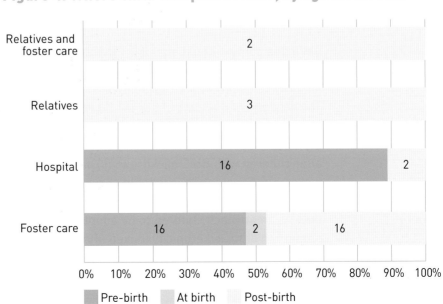

Source: Coram data (2000–2011); n=57

Gender, siblings and ethnicity of Coram Concurrent Planning children and adopted children (England)

Of the 57 children placed with Coram Concurrent Planning carers, 29 were girls and 28 boys. Fifty-three children were referred to the service as lone children, with a further two sibling groups referred, i.e. two birth mothers with two children each. The ethnicity of Coram Concurrent Planning children is shown in the table below, alongside the figures for looked after children who were adopted in England in 2011.

Table 1: Characteristics of children being adopted

Cohort	White % (n)	Mixed % (n)	Asian/ Asian British % (n)	Black/ Black British % (n)	Other ethnic groups % (n)
Coram Concurrent Planning	84% (48)	12% (7)	0% (0)	4% (2)	0% (0)
LAC adopted (England)	85% (2,930)	10% (330)	2% (60)	3% (90)	1% (30)
LAC (England)	78% (52,050)	9% (5,960)	4% (2,820)	7% (4,510)	2% (1,290)
LAC (London)	41% (4,220)	16% (1,650)	12% (1,210)	28% (2,880)	4% (380)

Source: Coram data (2000–2011); England data, DfE (2012), data were unavailable for a further 1% of LAC; London data, DfE (2011). Percentages have been rounded up.

Set in the context of national data, the Coram Concurrent Planning scheme has placed a comparable proportion of children with a Black and Minority Ethnic (BME) background as is placed for adoption nationally. The concurrent planning children adopted also reflect the national patterns in adoption – children with a BME background who are adopted are under-represented when compared with the proportion of looked after children with BME backgrounds, particularly relative to the London looked after population (see table above). However, as found nationally, it is notable that children with mixed ethnicity are much more likely than Asian or Black children to be adopted, and more in line with the proportion of mixed ethnicity looked after children.

Age of children at adoption order

On average, children adopted through the concurrent planning project were less than 17 months old when adopted (ranging from under seven months to just over three years old, n=52). Twenty-seven per cent (14) of children placed through the Coram Concurrent Planning Service were adopted before their first birthday. Nationally, in 2012, only two per cent (70) of children were adopted before they were a year old (DfE, 2012e).

Figure 5: Age of children at adoption order

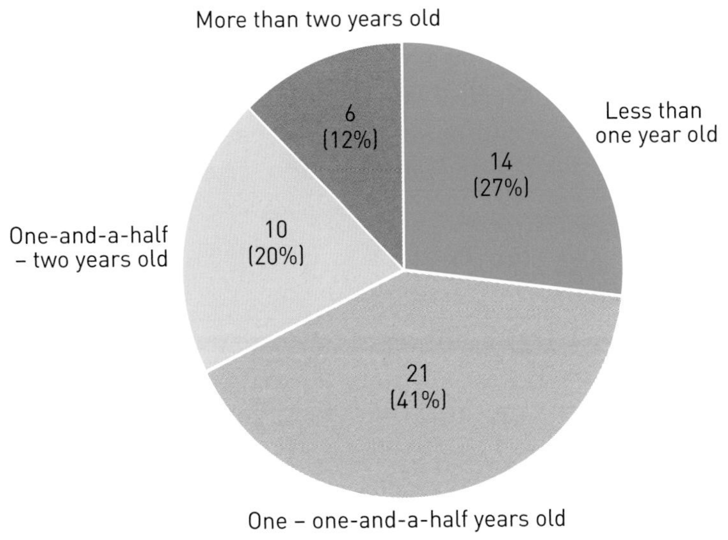

Source: Coram data (2000–2011); n=51

Adoption timescales

A goal of all adoption agencies is, of course, to complete the process of adoption in a timely way. Drawing on adoption scorecard data, it is possible to make some comparisons to national averages and to those local authorities most regularly referring children to the Coram Concurrent Planning Service.

The first scorecard indicator measures the average time it takes for a child who goes on to be adopted from entering care to moving in with her or his adoptive family. The target is set at 21 months (639 days). All children with data available who were adopted through concurrent planning met the national scorecard target and waited less than 21 months between entering care and moving in with their adoptive family. This comparison refers to the timescale to placement order, which takes less than nine months on average for Coram Concurrent Planning, but concurrent planning children were actually living with their carer, in a fostering placement, well before that point. Nationally, 56 per cent of children waited less than 21 months (Department for Education, 2012e).

We can also compare the length of care proceedings for the Coram Concurrent Planning group and national data. Care proceedings took less than 37 weeks on average for children adopted through the Coram Concurrent Planning Service (based on time taken from interim care order to final order), whereas it is 53 weeks nationally, for children of all ages (DfE scorecard 2012).

Table 2: Adoption scorecard comparisons

Cohort	Average time between a child entering care and moving in with their adoptive family, for children who have been adopted (days)*	Children who wait less than 21 months between entering care and moving in with their adoptive family (% and number)	Average length of care proceedings locally (to nearest whole week)
Coram Concurrent Planning Service (all under one year old)	262* (n=48)	100% (n=48)	37 (n=52)
England (2009–2012, all ages)	636	56% (10,180)	53
Camden (2009–2012, all ages)	542	62% (35)	54
Harrow (2009–2012, all ages)	635	85% (30)	51
Islington (2009–2012, all ages)	813	51% (30)	58

Source: Coram data (2000–2011) and adoption scorecards (DfE, 2012).
Note that the concurrent planning children will also be counted in national and partner local authorities' scorecard data.

The final stage of the adoption process is also quicker for Coram Concurrent Planning children, relative to national data. It takes a little over six months (190 days) to move from an adoptive placement to an adoption order for the Coram Concurrent Planning children on average, compared with nine months nationally in 2012 (six months for under-ones; DfE, 2012 data).

Figure 6: Number of days to adoptive placement and adoption order

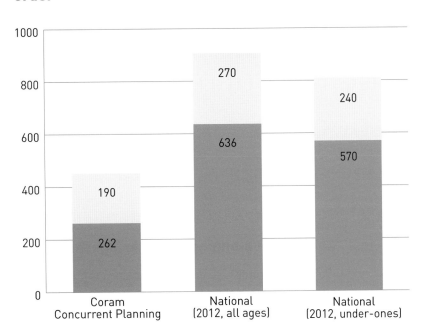

Entry to care (or first hearing) to adoptive placement (final order for Coram Concurrent Planning)

Adoptive placement (final order for Coram Concurrent Planning) to adoption order

Source: Coram Concurrent Planning entry to care/first hearing to adoptive placement (final order), n=48; Coram Concurrent Planning adoptive placement (final order) to adoption order, n=52; national data, all ages entry to care to adoptive placement; all other data (DfE scorecard Nov 2012).

Later in 2013, Coram will publish more detailed information on the outcomes for children placed through concurrent planning, based on in-depth interviews with adopters or the child's primary caregiver (where the child returned home), as well as Strengths and Difficulties Questionnaire data obtained from adopters (or primary caregivers) and teachers. Coram will examine the early experiences of children placed through the Coram Concurrent Planning Service, timescale and placement histories (including permanency outcomes and placement stability), health and behaviour, family and peer relations, school life and the experiences of adopters.

(These data have been reproduced with the kind permission of Coram Policy and Research Unit.)

Appendix 3
Cambridgeshire County Council: information for prospective carers

Concurrent planning in Cambridgeshire

We are looking for people who can care for, and then potentially adopt, some of the very young children in our care as part of the concurrent planning process which we are starting to implement in Cambridgeshire.

We work in partnership with Coram, a national children's charity and specialist voluntary adoption agency, which has been implementing concurrent planning since 1999.

What is concurrent planning?

Concurrent planning involves placing babies and young children under the age of two with special foster carers while the courts decide whether or not they can return to their birth families. These babies may be placed direct from hospital after birth if the court decides that they cannot go home without a full assessment. During this time the children will need to see their parents regularly and the concurrent carers will need to support the birth family's efforts to regain the care for their child.

Concurrent carers are approved as adopters as well as foster carers by Cambridgeshire adoption and permanence panel. When children are first placed, they are fostered by concurrent carers.

What is the role of concurrent carers?

While caring for the child placed with them, the concurrent carers will take the baby for regular contact with his or her parents several times a week. If the courts decide that the birth parents have shown they can be reliable, able and loving parents, the babies will be returned to their care. The concurrent carers will have the satisfaction of knowing that they have given these children the best possible start in life by providing care and security from the earliest time, and will help them settle back into their family.

However, if the courts decide that the child's parents cannot provide the security and care they need, and there are no alternative carers, the baby will remain with their concurrent carers and be adopted by them. We expect that this will be the most likely outcome in many of our concurrent planning cases.

What are the benefits of this approach?

The great advantage for the babies and young children is that it speeds up the planning for their lives. If they cannot go back to their birth family, it will avoid the stressful upheaval for the child when moving from foster home to a new adoptive family. They will have bonded with their adopted family from a very early age.

The advantage for the concurrent carers who go on to adopt is that they will have got to know their children from a very young age. They will also have had the opportunity to get to know their child's parents and will be in a good position to understand their background and struggles, which will be helpful for them and their adopted child in the future.

Who can be a concurrent carer?

We are looking for families who are resourceful and emotionally mature, able to put the needs of babies and young children first, and who can respect and work with children's families in the early months. We need families from different backgrounds and religions, single parents as well as couples. It is important that families have a strong support network to rely on.

We expect that many of the concurrent carers will go on to adopt the children they have cared for and helped through the early, unsettling months when plans were still uncertain.

What support do concurrent carers receive?

Concurrent carers will be offered special training and workshops to prepare them for the task. Our dedicated team of experienced social workers offer ongoing high quality support to families and children. We also provide ongoing post-adoption support and a comprehensive range of continuing training opportunities.

The carers will receive fostering allowances during the period the children are fostered.

What is the next stage for potential concurrent carers?

You can contact us on .... for an informal chat with the duty adoption social worker.

For more information about the adoption application process, please go to:

Website...

Phone....

February 2013

(Reproduced with the kind permission of Cambridgeshire Council Council.)

Appendix 4
Cambridgeshire County Council: information for parents

Most parents reading this leaflet will not have their child living with them, or will know that the local authority plan is for your baby to be looked after by foster carers. The court will be making decisions about your child's future and you may be feeling angry, sad or confused. You are probably worried about what is going to happen to your child in care. This leaflet provides information about involving you as a parent in planning for your child's future.

Concurrent planning

Concurrent planning is a new way of working with families. It is a programme to help parents and their children in situations where there are care proceedings and long-term plans for the children need to be made. The aim is to reduce the number of moves and changes children experience while living away from their parent(s) to make sure that your child has the best possible care while his or her long-term future is decided.

Staying in a temporary foster home is not always good for young children, especially if they have to move several times while waiting for decisions to be made. This is bound to make it more difficult for a child to settle when the court makes a decision, whether they return to their parents' care, go to relatives or are later placed for adoption.

The concurrent planning programme in Cambridgeshire offers young children a different experience. Our main concern is the wellbeing of your child, and if possible we would like him or her to return to live with you. The next choice is for your child to be cared for by another relative. While these two possibilities are being explored, the programme offers your child a placement with a specially prepared family who are approved both as foster carers and as adopters. These families are committed to helping us to reunite parents with their children if this is possible. However, if the court decides that your child cannot return home to you or another member of your family, these special carers are ready to offer the child the security of adoption without facing another move.

What we will offer you as parents

- We will complete a pre-birth assessment, but we will not be carrying out a further parenting assessment unless this is ordered by the court. The court will decide what other assessments you need to have, if any, and when reports must be completed by so that there are no unnecessary delays.

- We will provide a written agreement setting out the contact arrangements, what you are expected to do and what help is available for you.

- We will provide opportunities for contact with your child in one of our contact centres with our concurrent planning contact supervisor. The decision about how often you see your child is made in court.

- We will provide opportunities to develop parenting skills.

- We will provide help with any practical arrangements.

What could happen to your child?

The court will decide whether your child can return to you or another member of your family. The decision will be based on the evidence from you and the assessment reports, as well as evidence from social workers, the Children's Guardian, and any other professional who has been asked to do an assessment or give an opinion.

If the court decides that your child cannot return to you or a member of your extended family, then the best plan will be for your child to have the security of adoption by people who are already familiar to you and your child. This would avoid an upsetting move for your child. You would already know the carers and we hope you would feel confident that they would give your child the love and security he or she needs. We hope that you would also feel that the carers respect and understand you and will be able to tell the child later that you loved him or her, but that you had some problems which made it difficult for you to look after them.

The carers will be specially selected and trained

It will be their job to help to support you by keeping the relationship going with your child. You will be able to meet them and get to know them when they bring your child to contact. They will be able to tell you what is happening to your child and what progress he or she is making.

The professionals

Your social worker will be happy to explain in more detail the information in this leaflet. You may also find it helpful to discuss the leaflet with your solicitor.

We would be very pleased to meet you and answer your questions about concurrent planning. You can contact us on free phone number .... and ask to speak to the Duty Adoption Social Worker who will arrange an appointment.

February 2013

(Reproduced with the kind permission of Cambridgeshire Council Council.)

Appendix 5
Cambridgeshire County Council: concurrent planning contact agreement

Concurrent planning contact agreement for parents and carers

SUPERVISED CONTACT TEAM

Team address	
Telephone number	

Family name	
Agreement date	Venue
Referrer	
Team	
Supervising contact worker	
Present	Role

Why has supervised contact been requested? (Legal status and care plans)

What will be observed/documented?

- Parent'(s) sensitivity to the baby's mood and ability to respond appropriately.

- Parent'(s) ability to remain focused on contact and not be distracted by phone, issues or problems parents may have outside of contact.

- Parent'(s) ability to remain positive and not speak negatively about the absent parent, carer or any other professionals.

- Parent'(s) ability to anticipate and respond to the baby's needs, putting these before her/his own.

- Parent'(s) ability to engage and stimulate the baby with age-appropriate talk and activities.

- Parent'(s) ability to hold the baby correctly when feeding, or in general, ability to complete tasks like nappy changing, winding, etc.

- Parent'(s) ability to settle the baby, if she or he is fretful or crying, demonstrating that the parent is able to eliminate various possible causes: wet nappy, too hot, etc.

- Parent'(s) ability to accept advice from the contact supervisor and learn about appropriate ways of responding to the baby.

Interventions by contact supervisor

- If the parent becomes distracted from contact.

- If the parent initiates negative talk about the absent parent, carer or any other professional.

- Suggest or demonstrate a more effective way of performing a task, e.g. feeding, winding, nappy changing, or holding baby, etc.

- Help the parent to settle the baby, supervisor may make suggestions or demonstrate a more effective way. If the baby is unable to settle, "time out" is offered. If contact does not appear to be in the baby's interest, the session will be ended.

- If the parent(s) displays aggressive and volatile behaviour, physically or verbally, contact will be cancelled.

- If the parent(s) appear to be under the influence of alcohol or drugs, contact will be cancelled.

- In all cases where contact has to be cancelled due to a safeguarding concern, a review of contact will take place before recommencing.

Level of supervision required?

The contact supervisor remains in sight and sound of the child and parents at all times.

Are supervised outings in the community permissible?

Who will be present during contact?

Contact arrangements

- Contact will start on xx, after that it will take place on x days from xx to xx.

- Location of contact will take place at xx.

- Contact will be reviewed with parents, the child's social worker and contact supervisor at monthly intervals.

- Handovers:
  Arrivals: 5–10 minutes allowance for handovers to take place and parent(s) to receive feedback from the carer on their child's development. This is also an opportunity for the parent(s) to ask relevant questions pertaining to their child's general development, i.e. feeding and sleeping patterns.
  Departures: carers will leave with the child after they have received feedback from the parent(s). Parent(s) will wait 15 minutes before leaving to ensure the carers have vacated the premises and left the area.

- This time will be an opportunity for the parent(s) and supervisor to review progress of contact.

- A communication book will be provided by the carer(s) detailing basic information on the child's care day and night, how well she or he fed or slept.

- Photos may not be taken during contact. However, photos may be provided by the contact supervisor who will take photos during contact.

- Photographs may not be shared on Facebook or any other social network.

- Mobile phones may not be used during contact.

- Support is offered throughout contact; however, if the parent(s) requires additional support, the supervisor will refer them to the social worker.

What will happen if the parents do not arrive for contact and do not call the Supervised Contact Team to say they will be late?

On the day of contact, if the parent(s) do not call or arrive within 15 minutes of contact start time, contact will be cancelled and not replaced. It would be unfair on the baby to wait indefinitely, which could cause unnecessary anxiety and stress.

If the parent(s) have failed to attend two contacts without giving prior notice, they will for future contacts be required to phone the contact supervisor, at a time previously agreed, before the start of contact to confirm their attendance, or the carers will be informed that contact is cancelled for that day to prevent the baby travelling unnecessarily.

If the parent(s) phone in to say that they are delayed, the carers and child will wait 30 minutes (inclusive of handover time), but contact is not extended to compensate for a late arrival by parent(s).

Supervised Contact Team Duty number:

What the parent/carer may be responsible for (e.g. bottles, nappies, snacks)

Carers will provide all essential items in an appropriate baby bag, e.g. bottles, nappies, etc.

Parent(s) are encouraged to provide toys for contact.

Transport arrangements and plans in place

- The parent(s) may be accompanied by their social worker on the first occasion.
- The parent(s) will make their own way for subsequent contact.
- Financial assistance will be provided if necessary.

Risks identified

See risk assessment.

Expectations of parent(s)

- To keep to the plans made in the Agreement; this includes the beginning and ending of the contact session.

- To not be verbally or physically aggressive.

- To notify the supervised contact team if you are delayed or unable to attend contact as soon as possible, and no later than within 15 minutes of the start time.

- Only those specified in this Agreement may attend the contact session.

- To appreciate that the contact supervisor has no responsibility for social work or legal decision making, but will share their observations with other professionals.

- To ensure any new phone numbers are passed to the contact supervisor or the social worker at the earliest possible convenience.

Expectations of the carer(s)

- To keep to the plans made in the Agreement.

- To notify the supervised contact team if you are unable to attend contact as soon as possible, and at least within 15 minutes of the start time.

- To ensure all essential items for contact are provided.

- To engage with the baby's parents during handovers in a calm and friendly manner.

- To respect the parents as the child's parents and to consult and inform them as appropriate.

- To ensure any new phone numbers are passed to the contact supervisor or social worker at the soonest possible convenience.

Expectations of your social work unit

- Will always be present at the first contact and will attend at least 20 per cent of contacts.

- To ensure any changes such as addresses and phone numbers are passed to the supervised contact team as soon as possible.

- To ensure any changes to the contact such as venues, times or persons present (family or professionals) are passed to the supervised contact team at the earliest possible time.

Expectations of the supervised contact team:

- We will work with you to ensure your time with your child is a happy experience.

- To ensure we keep to the days, times and venues agreed.

- Should your child be unwell and the contact session needs to be cancelled, we will contact you as soon as possible.

- Should your contact supervisor be unable to undertake the contact, we will let you know and if possible find another supervisor.

- We will try to ensure you have the same room for each session.

- The supervised contact team are available should you wish to discuss your views and comments about the service we are providing.

- To make recordings following each contact session that will be sent to the referring social worker. These will be used in reports to court.

Honesty/openness

- The supervised contact team agrees to work in partnership, in an honest and open manner, sharing concerns with individuals/family as well as positive things.

- All work will be shared with the referring social worker.

- Contact reports will be shared with the parents via court proceedings.

Concerns

- Individuals, families and carers have a right to raise concerns about the service. If you are unhappy with the service, please speak to your contact supervisor. If you are still unhappy, ask to speak to the manager.

- We welcome feedback on our service and rely on this to make improvements. At a later date we will be asking you to provide feedback on the service and hope you will agree to do this.

Name and contact details for contact manager:

Telephone number:

Agreement signed by

Parent/s	
Carer/s	
Child's social worker	Carer's social worker
Manager/Deputy Manager Supervised Contact Team	

(Reproduced with the kind permission of Cambridgeshire Council Council.)

Appendix 6
Concurrent planning referral and care planning flowchart

This flowchart should be adapted depending on local authority decision-making protocols.

Referral into local authority social work team
Initial assessment

Core assessment/pre-birth assessment
(Background history/chronology/genogram)
Information given to parents about concurrent planning as appropriate

Referral for Family Group Conference/Family Network Meeting – consider potential role of family and friends – information given to wider FGC about concurrent planning as appropriate

Decision making about PLO pre-proceedings meetings/Legal strategy meeting
Notification to CAFCASS as appropriate

Details of concurrent planning discussed fully with parents
Written information given to parents and their lawyers

Pre-birth child protection conference

Referral for concurrent placement and management decision about appropriateness of initiating care proceedings and of a concurrent care plan
Decision made about appropriate potential concurrent placement and reasons for this fully recorded

Social work meetings with prospective carers to provide information about potential placement/meeting with appropriate medical adviser set up

If plan for interim care order (ICO) at birth – all appropriate staff advised – recorded on birth plan with hospital staff

ICO application/initial court hearing and decision made about local authority care plan for a concurrent placement

Transition planning meetings/meeting between parents and concurrent carers ideally prior to first contact meeting
Child placed with concurrent carers under fostering regulations

Parents meet with contact supervisor/set up agreements about contact
Contact and other assessment work agreed within court framework continues

Progress of assessment work and contact kept under regular review
Parents and carers informed as appropriate – provision of additional support/counselling for parents and for carers as required

Decision of agency decision maker about whether child should be placed for adoption or not. If rehabilitation is the plan, supervision and support plan agreed

Final hearing if adoption is plan and placement order obtained

↓

Adoption and permanence panel recommends the match for adoption

↓

ADM ratifies panel recommendation

↓

Placement becomes adoptive placement

Bibliography

Adams P (2012) *Planning for Contact in Permanent Placements*, London: BAAF

Ainsworth MDS, Blehar MC, Waters E and Wall S (1978) *Patterns of Attachment: A psychological study of the Strange Situation,* Hillsdale, NJ: Erlbaum

Argent H and Coleman J (2012) *Dealing with Disruption*, London: BAAF

Association of Directors of Children's Services (ADCS) (2013) *Adoption Data Analysis: Full report with executive summary*, London: Policy Intelligence

Barlow J and Underdown A (2008) 'Attachment and infant development', in Jackson C, Hill K and Lavis P (eds) *Child and Adolescent Mental Health Today,* Brighton: Pavilion Publishing/Mental Health Foundation

Biehal N, Ellison S, Baker C and Sinclair I (2010) *Belonging and Permanence: Outcomes in long-term foster care and adoption*, London: BAAF

Brennan K, Szolnocki J and Horn M (2003) *Lutheran Community Services Concurrent Planning Evaluation: Stuart Foundation final report*, Seattle, WA: Northwest Institute for Children and Families (NICF), University of Washington School of Social Work, accessed 13 March 2013, at web. archive.org/web/20040630115407/http://depts.washington.edu/nwicf/ EvalServ/LCS%20Final%20Report.pdf

Calder MC (2003) 'Unborn children: a framework for assessment and intervention', in Calder MC and Hackett S (eds) *Assessment in Child Care: Using and developing frameworks for practice*, Lyme Regis: Russell House Publishing, pp. 362–374

Child Welfare Information Gateway (2012) *Concurrent Planning: What the evidence shows*, Washington, DC: US Department of Health and Human Services, accessed 13 March 2013, at www.childwelfare.gov/pubs/issue_ briefs/concurrent_evidence/concurrent_evidence.pdf

Coram (undated) *Coram Concurrent Planning Project: Information for carers*, available at: www.coram.org.uk/assets/downloads/Concurrent_ Planning_Leaflet-_For_Carers1.pdf

Chugani DC, Muzik O, Behan M; Rothermel R *et al* (2001) 'Developmental changes in brain serotonin synthesis capacity in autistic and nonautisistic children', *Annals of Neurology*, 45:3, pp. 287–295

Dale P (2011, unpublished) *Restrictions on Natural Parent Contact with Infants during Care Proceedings: Some cautions about recent research and developing practice*, accessed 13 March 2013 at www.peterdale.co.uk/wp-content/uploads/2011/08/ContactPaper2011.pdf

D'Andrade A, Frame L and Duerr Berrick J (2006) 'Concurrent planning in public child welfare agencies: oxymoron or work in progress?', *Children and Youth Services Review*, 28:1, pp. 78–95

Davies C and Ward H (2011) *Safeguarding Children across Services: Messages from research on identifying and responding to child maltreatment: Executive summary*, London: Department for Education, accessed 13 March 2013 at www.education.gov.uk/publications/eOrderingDownload/DFE-RBX-10-09.pdf

Department for Education (2012a) *An Action Plan for Adoption: Tackling delay*, London: Department for Education, accessed 13 March 2013 at www.education.gov.uk/publications/eOrderingDownload/action%20plan%20for%20adoption.pdf

Department for Education (2012b) *Adoption and Fostering: Tackling delay: Consultation paper*, London: Department for Education, accessed 13 March 2013 at www.education.gov.uk/consultations/index.cfm?action=conResults&consultationId=1853&external=no&menu=3

Department for Education (2012c) *Proposals for Placing Children with their Potential Adopters Earlier*, London: Department for Education, accessed 13 March 2013 at www.media.education.gov.uk/assets/files/pdf/p/proposals%20for%20earlier%20placement%20of%20children%20with%20their%20potential%20adopters.pdf

Department for Education (2012d) *More Babies in Care to Receive a Stable Home More Swiftly* (press release), accessed 13 March 2013 at www.education.gov.uk/inthenews/inthenews/a00211426/more-babies-in-care-to-receive-a-stable-home-more-swiftly-

Department for Education (2012e) *Adoption Scorecards*, available at www.education.gov.uk/childrenandyoungpeople/families/adoption/a00208817/adoption-scorecards

Department for Education (2013) *Further Action on Adoption: Finding more loving homes*, London: Department for Education, accessed 13 March 2013 at https://www.education.gov.uk/publications/eOrderingDownload/Further%20Action%20on%20Adoption.pdf

Fahlberg V (1994) *A Child's Journey through Placement*, London: BAAF

Family Justice Review Panel (2011) *Family Justice Review: Final report*, London: Ministry of Justice

Farmer E (2009) 'Reunification with birth families,' in Schofield G and Simmonds J (eds) *The Child Placement Handbook: Research, theory and practice*, London: BAAF, pp. 83–101

Farmer E and Lutman E (2012) *Effective Working with Neglected Children and their Families: Linking interventions to long-term outcomes*, London: Jessica Kingsley Publishers

Farmer E, Sturgess W, O'Neill T and Wijedasa D (2011) *Achieving Successful Returns from Care: What makes reunification work?* London, BAAF

Frame L, Duerr Berrick J and Foulkes Coakley J (2006) 'Essential elements of implementing a system of concurrent planning', *Child and Family Social Work*, 11:4, pp. 357–367

Gerhardt S (2004) *Why Love Matters: How affection shapes a baby's brain*, Hove: Brunner-Routledge

Gerstenzang S and Freundlich M (2005) 'A critical assessment of concurrent planning in New York State', *Adoption Quarterly*, 8:4, pp. 1–22

Hart D (2001) 'Assessment before birth', in Howarth J (ed) *The Child's World: Assessing children in need*, London: Jessica Kingsley Publishers

Haugaard JJ, Wojslawowicz JC and Palmer M (1999) 'Outcomes in adolescent and older-child adoptions', *Adoption Quarterly*, 3:1, pp. 61–69

Haynes P (2003) *Managing Complexity in the Public Services*, Maidenhead: Open University Press

Hill C and Edwards M (2009) 'Birth family health history: adopters' perspectives on learning about their child's health inheritance', *Adoption & Fostering*, 33:2, pp. 45–53

Hodges J, Steel M, Hillman S, Henderson K, Kanuik J (2003) 'Changes in attachment representations over the first year of adoptive placement: narratives of maltreated children', *Clinical Child Psychology and Psychiatry*, 8, pp. 351–367

Howe D (2009) 'The impact of histories of abuse and neglect on children in placement', in Schofield G and Simmonds J (eds) *The Child Placement Handbook: Research, theory and practice*, London: BAAF, pp. 47–62

Humphreys C and Kiraly M (2011) 'High-frequency family contact: a road to nowhere for infants', *Child and Family Social Work*, 16:1, pp. 1–11

Jones DPH (1991) 'The effectiveness of intervention', in Adcock M and White R (eds) *Significant Harm: Its management and outcome*, London: Significant Publications, pp. 61–84

Jones DPH (1998) 'The effectiveness of intervention', in Adcock M and White R (eds) *Significant Harm: Its management and outcome* (2nd edition), London: Significant Publications, pp. 91–119

Juffer F and Van IJzendoorn MH (2005) 'Behaviour problems and mental health referrals of international adoptees: a meta-analysis'. *JAMA - The Journal of the American Medical Association*, 293, pp. 2501–2515

Juffer F and Van IJzendoorn MH (2007) 'Adoptees do not lack self-esteem: a meta-analysis of studies on self-esteem of transracial, international, and domestic adoptees', *Psychological Bulletin*, 133, pp. 1067–1083

Katz L (1996a) 'Permanency action through concurrent planning', *Adoption & Fostering*, 20:2, pp. 8–13

Katz L (1996b) 'Concurrent planning: fifteen years later', *Adoptalk*, Spring, pp. 12–13

Katz L (1999) 'Concurrent planning: benefits and pitfalls', *Child Welfare*, 78:1, pp. 71–87

Katz L, Spoonemore N and Robinson C (1994) *Concurrent Planning: From permanency planning to permanency action*, Seattle, WA: Lutheran Social Services of Washington and Idaho

Kelly G, Haslett P, O'Hare J and McDowell K (2007) 'Permanence planning in Northern Ireland: a development project', *Adoption & Fostering*, 31:3, pp. 18–27

Kenrick J (2009) 'Concurrent planning: a retrospective study of the continuities and discontinuities of care, and their impact on the development of infants and young children placed for adoption by the Coram Concurrent Planning Project', *Adoption & Fostering*, 33:4, pp. 5–18

Laws S, Wilson R and Rabindrakumar S (2012) *Concurrent Planning Study Interim Report*, London: Coram

Mather M (2004) 'Finding out about the past to understand the present: working with the medical adviser in adoption and foster care', in Phillips R (eds) *Children Exposed to Parental Substance Misuse: Implications for family placement*, London: BAAF, pp. 15–29

Mitchell LB, Barth RP, Green R, Wall A, Biemer P, Berrick JD, Webb MB and the National Survey of Child and Adolescent Well-Being Research Group (2005) 'Child welfare reform in the United States: findings from a local agency survey', *Child Welfare*, 84:1, pp. 5–24

Monck E, Reynolds J and Wigfall V (2003) *The Role of Concurrent Planning: Making permanent placements for young children*, London: BAAF

Munby, Lord Justice (2010) *President of the Family Division/Family Justice Council Debate, 8th December 2010: Contact for Babies in Care Proceedings*, pp. 21–25, accessed 13 March 2013 at www.baaf.org.uk/webfm_send/2117

Music G (2011) *Nurturing Natures: Attachment and children's emotional, sociocultural and brain development*, Hove: Psychology Press

North California Training Academy (2009) *Concurrent Planning: Existing challenges and new possibilities*, Davis, CA: Centre for Human Services

Northwest Resource Center for Children and Families at University of Washington (2003) *Concurrent Planning Evaluation, Stuart Foundation Final Report*, Seattle, WA: Northwest Resource Center for Children and Families at University of Washington School of Social Work

Perry B (2008) *Bonding and Attachment in Maltreated Children: Consequences of emotional neglect in childhood*, accessed 25 January 2010, available at: http://teacher.scholastic.com/professional/bruceperry/index.htm.

Phillips R (ed) (2004) *Children Exposed to Parental Substance Misuse: Implications for family placement*, London: BAAF

Plant M (2004) 'Parental alcohol misuse: implications for child placements', in Phillips R (ed) *Children Exposed to Parental Substance Misuse: Implications for family placement*, London: BAAF, pp. 73–85

Potter M, The Rt Hon Sir, President of the Family Division (2006) 'Achieving best outcomes for babies in the care system', *Family Law*, 36, pp. 1036–1040

Quinton D (2012) *Rethinking Matching in Adoptions from Care*, London: BAAF

Rushton A and Dance C (2004) 'The outcomes of late permanent placements: the adolescent years', *Adoption & Fostering*, 28:1, pp. 49–58

Schofield G and Beek M (2006) *Attachment Handbook for Foster Care and Adoption*, London: BAAF

Schofield G and Simmonds J (2011) 'Contact for infants subject to care proceedings', *Adoption & Fostering*, 35:4, pp. 70–74

Selwyn J, Sturgess W, Quinton D and Baxter C (2006) *Costs and Outcomes of Non-Infant Adoptions*, London: BAAF

Simmonds J (2009) 'Adoption: developmental perspectives within an ethical, legal and policy framework', in Schofield G and Simmonds J (eds) *The Child Placement Handbook: Research, policy and practice*, London: BAAF, pp. 220–240

Simmonds J (2013) *Fostering for Adoption: Practice guidance*, London: Coram and BAAF, available at: www.coram.org.uk/section/Fostering-for-adoption-guidance

Van den Dries L, Juffer F, Van IJzendoorn MH and Bakermans-Kranenburg MJ (2009) 'Fostering security? A meta-analysis of attachment in adopted children', *Children and Youth Services Review*, 31:3, pp. 410–421

Van IJzendoorn MH, Schuengel C and Bakermans-Kranenburg MJ (1999) 'Disorganised attachment in early childhood: meta-analysis of precursors, concomitants, and sequelae', *Development and Psychopathology, 11,* pp. 225–249

Wand GS, McCaul ME, Gotjen D, Reynolds J and Lee S (2001) 'Confirmation that offspring from families with alcohol-dependent individuals have greater Hypothalamic-Pituitary-Adrenal Axis Activation induced by Naloxone compared with offspring without a family history of alcohol dependence', *Alcoholism: Clinical and Experimental Research,* 25, pp. 1134–1139

Ward H, Munro ER and Dearden C (2006) *Babies and Young Children in Care: Life pathways, decision-making and practice,* London: Jessica Kingsley Publishers

Ward H, Brown R and Westlake D (2012) *Safeguarding Babies and Very Young Children from Abuse and Neglect,* London: Jessica Kingsley

Wigfalll V, Monck E and Reynolds J (2006) 'Putting programme into practice: the introduction of concurrent planning into mainstream adoption and fostering services', *British Journal of Social Work,* 36:1, pp. 41–55

ACTS, REGULATIONS, STANDARDS AND GUIDANCE

Acts
Children Act 1989
Adoption and Children Act 2002
Children Act 2004

Bills
Children and Families Bill 2013

Regulations
Adoption Agencies Regulations 2005
Adoption Agencies (Panel and Consequential Amendments) Regulations 2012
Fostering Services (England) Regulations 2011
Care Planning, Placement and Case Review (England) Regulations 2010
Care Planning, Placement and Case Review and Fostering Services (Miscellaneous Amendments) Regulations 2013

Standards
National Minimum Standards for Adoption (2011)
National Minimum Standards for Fostering (2011)

Guidance

Adoption and Children Act 2002, Adoption Statutory Guidance, first revision 2011

Children Act 1989 Guidance Volume 2: Care Planning, Placement and Case Review 2010

Update to the Children Act 1989 Guidance and Regulations Volume 2: Care Planning, Placement and Case Review (CPPR 2010)

Children Act 1989 Guidance Volume 4: Fostering Services 2011

Family and Friends Care: Statutory Guidance for Local Authorities 2011